THE 2014 RHYSLING ANTHOLOGY

Also available from the
Science Fiction Poetry Association

The Alchemy of Stars: Rhysling Award Winners Showcase
Edited by Roger Dutcher and Mike Allen

The 2013 Rhysling Anthology: The Best Science Fiction, Fantasy, and Horror Poetry of 2012
Edited by John C. Mannone

The 2012 Rhysling Anthology: The Best Science Fiction, Fantasy, and Horror Poetry of 2011
Edited by Lyn C. A. Gardner

The 2011 Rhysling Anthology: The Best Science Fiction, Fantasy, and Horror Poetry of 2010
Edited by David Lunde

Spec-Tacular: Fantasy Favorites From Raven Electrick Ink
Edited by Karen A. Romanko

Uncommonplaces: Poems of the Fantastic
Edited by Judith Kerman & Don Riggs

The Stars as Seen From This Particular Angle of Night: An Anthology of Speculative Verse
Edited by Sandra Kasturi

On the Wing: American Poems of Air and Space Flight
Edited by Karen Yelena Olsen

Voyagers
Edited by Mark Pirie & Tim Jones

Order from the **SFPA Bookstore**
astore.amazon.com/sfpoetry-20

Proceeds from the sale of *Confessions: A Nightmare in Five Acts* (Elektric Milk Bath Press, 2013) go to support SFPA.
Order from elektrikmilkbathpress.com/bookstore

THE 2014 RHYSLING ANTHOLOGY

THE BEST SCIENCE FICTION,
FANTASY, AND HORROR
POETRY OF 2013

SELECTED BY THE
SCIENCE FICTION
POETRY ASSOCIATION

EDITED BY
Elizabeth R. McClellan

ASSOCIATE
EDITOR
Ashley Brown

Copyright © 2014
by the Science Fiction Poetry Association
in the names of the individual contributors.
All works used by permission.

All rights to individual poems revert to authors or poem copyright holders. No part of this compilation may be reproduced in any form without permission in writing from the SFPA president, except in the case of brief quotations embodied in critical or analytical reviews or articles.

Editor and Rhysling Chair: Elizabeth R. McClellan
Associate Editor: Ashley Brown
Layout and Design: Christopher E. Johnson
Cover Design: David Lee Summers
Publisher: Science Fiction Poetry Association
Published in cooperation with: Hadrosaur Productions
SFPA President: Bryan D. Dietrich

About the cover: Image by Francis Reddy, courtesy of the StarChild project, a service of the High Energy Astrophysics Science Archive Research Center (HEASARC), within the Astrophysics Science Division (ASD) at the National Aeronautics and Space Administration (NASA) Goddard Space Flight Center. The artist's rendering is a conceptual image of the dwarf planet Eris and its only known moon, Dysnomia.

Cataloging-in-Publication Data

The 2014 Rhysling Anthology: the best science fiction, fantasy, and horror poetry of 2013 / selected by the Science Fiction Poetry Association; edited by Elizabeth R. McClellan.

    p. cm.
Includes bibliographical references.
ISBN 978-1-885093-77-6
1. Poetry. 2. Science fiction poetry. 3. Fantasy poetry. 4. Horror poetry.
I. McClellan, Elizabeth R., 1980–

For more information about the
Science Fiction Poetry Association,
visit www.sfpoetry.com

ACKNOWLEDGMENTS

Allen, Mike. "Hungry Constellations," *Goblin Fruit*, Fall 2013, goblinfruit.net/2013/fall/feature/.
Anderson, Leslie J. "The Captain Speaks," *Star*Line* 36.1.
Anderson, Leslie J. "Ponies and Rocketships," *Asimov's Science Fiction*, September 2013.
Arkenberg, Megan. "Songs at a Crossroads," *Ideomancer* 12.1, ideomancer.com/?p=2369.
Bergmann, F.J. "Nephology," *James Gunn's Ad Astra* 2, adastra.ku.edu/nephology/.
Bergmann, F.J. "What She Dreams Of," *ChiZine*, March 2013.
Berman, Ruth. "How Many," *Asimov's Science Fiction*, February 2013.
Blackford, Jenny. "Hungry as Living Sorrow," 2013 Science Fiction Poetry Association Contest, sfpoetry.com/contests/13contest.html.
Blackmore, Leigh. "The Last Dream," *Weird Fiction Review* 4.
Borski, Robert. "Liar, Liar," *Dreams and Nightmares* 94.
Boston, Bruce. "Living on the Leys," *Bête Noire* 12.
Boston, Bruce. "Music of the Stars," 2013 *Balticon Program Book*.
Bradley, Lisa M. "Riveted," *Flying Higher: An Anthology of Superhero Poetry*, eds. Michael Damian Thomas and Shira Lipkin (2013).
Bryant, Shelly. "View from the Oort Cloud," *Illumen*, Spring 2013.
Bundock, Rachael. "singing the plains," *Goblin Fruit*, Summer 2013, goblinfruit.net/2013/summer/poems/?poem=singingtheplains.
Clare, Gwendolyn. "The Narrow Hours," *Bull Spec* 8.
Clark, G. O. "Climbing Up the Sky," *Tales of the Talisman* 9.1, September 2013.
Clark, Jennifer. "Interim Problem Report 119V-0080," *Paper Crow* 3.1.
Clink, Carolyn. [untitled tanka], *Gusts: Contemporary Tanka* 18, Fall/Winter 2013, sfpoet.com/content/its-2014-already
Clink, David. "A City of Buried Rivers," *Literary Review of Canada*, Vol. 29, Issue 1, November 2013.
Crow, Jennifer. "Why I Sold My Soul to the Storyteller," *The First Bite of the Apple* (Elektrik Milk Bath Press, 2013).
Crowley, Jane. "Triptych," *Strange Horizons*, September 9, 2013, strangehorizons.com/2013/20130909/crowley-p.shtml.
Dorr, James S. "The Specialist," *Disturbed Digest*, June 2013.
Duthie, Peg. "The Bed I Haven't Made Yet," *Star*Line* 36.2.
El-Mohtar, Amal. "Turning the Leaves," *Apex Magazine* 55, apex-magazine.com/turning-the-leaves/.
Evans, Kendall. "Into the Deep," *James Gunn's Ad Astra* 2, adastra.ku.edu/into-the-deep/.
Frazier, Robert. "The Girl Who Tipped Through Time," 2013 Science Fiction Poetry Association Contest, sfpoetry.com/contests/13contest.html.
Frazier, Robert. "Your Clone and You," *Dreams and Nightmares* 94.
Gage, Joshua. "imagining," *INHUMAN: Haiku from the Zombie Apocalypse* (The Poet's Haven, 2013).
Gardner, Adele. "Diana's Justice," *Heroic Fantasy Quarterly* 16, April 1, 2013, heroicfantasyquarterly.com/?p=1375.
Gardner, Adele. "Wheels," *Mythic Delirium* 28, Winter/Spring 2013.
Hightower, Nancy. "A Virtuous Woman," *Prick of the Spindle* Vol. 7.3, September 2013, prickofthespindle.com/poetry/7.3/hightower/virtuous.html.
Hoffmann, Ada. "The Siren of Mayberry Crescent," *Mythic Delirium* 29.
Jones, Russell. "After the Moons," *Spaces of Their Own* (Stewed Rhubarb Press, 2013).

Kindred, Sally Rosen. "Gingerbread House: The Apron's Lot," *Jabberwock Review*, Winter 2013.
Kindred, Sally Rosen. "Sleeping Beauty Makes Dinner," *Goblin Fruit*, Winter 2013, goblinfruit.net/2013/winter/poems/?poem=sleepingbeautymakesdinner.
Kopaska-Merkel, David C. "Backwater," *The Magazine of Speculative Poetry*, Fall 2013.
Kopaska-Merkel, David C. and Kendall Evans, "The Bagel Shop Across the Street," *Not One of Us* 50.
Kozma, Andrew. "Pinocchio in the Toothpick Factory," *Star*Line* 36.2.
Landis, Geoffrey A. "Across the Dark, the Pioneers," *Starship Century: Toward the Grandest Horizon*, eds. James Benford and Gregory Benford (Microwave Sciences, 2013).
Landis, Geoffrey A. "Rivers," *Asimov's Science Fiction*, June 2013.
Lane, Dennis M. "The Waiting," *The Ghazal Page*, November 2013.
Lee, B.J. "Don't Call Me A Fairy," *Spellbound*, Spring 2013.
Lee, Mary Soon. "Interregnum," *Star*Line* 36.4, sfpoetry.com/sl/edchoice/36.4-3.html.
Lemberg, Rose. "I will show you a single treasure from the treasures of Shah Niyaz," *Goblin Fruit*, Summer 2013, goblinfruit.net/2013/summer/poems/?poem=asingletreasure.
Light, John C. "Doppelgänger," *AWEN* 82, November 2013.
Lindow, Sandra J. "Timeline Tapestry," *A Wisconsin Harvest* Vol. II.
Lindow, Sandra J. "Topic of Cancer," 2014 *Wisconsin Poets' Calendar*.
Lindsey, Darrell. "Leaving Papa," *Kaleidotrope* Summer 2013, kaleidotrope.net/archives/summer-2013/leaving-papa-by-darrell-lindsey/.
Marshall, Helen. "Bluebeard's Wife," *The Sex Lives of Monsters* (Kelp Queen Press, 2013).
Marshall, Helen. "The Collected Postcards of Billy the Kid," *Postscripts to Darkness* 4.
Matthews, Jason. "Special Delivery from the Unnamed Quadrant," *Star*Line* 36.2.
McMyne, Mary. "Irène Joliot-Curie," *Painted Bride Quarterly* 86, February 2013.
Odasso, Adrienne J. "Heaven and Earth," *Niteblade*, December 2013, niteblade.com/home/december-2013/2013/12/01/heaven-earth/.
Odasso, Adrienne J. "Ivy," *Not One of Us* 50.
Odasso, Adrienne J. "Rigel," *Dark Mountain Book* 4.
Parisien, Dominik. "Sand Bags," *Strange Horizons*, November 18, 2013, strangehorizons.com/2013/20131118/parisien-p.shtml.
Qyn. "Ophelia," *Strange Horizons*, May 20, 2013, strangehorizons.com/2013/20130520/qyn-p.shtml.
Relf, Terrie Leigh. "While on the evacuation shuttle," *Star*Line* 36.4.
Robertson, S. Brackett. "Rhythm of Hoof and Cry," *Mythic Delirium* 0.1, mythicdelirium.com/?page_id=423.
Rowe, James Frederick William. "The Bone-Cutter's Lament," *Songs of Eretz* 1.2, eretzsongs.blogspot.com/p/e-zine_4.html.
Samatar, Sofia. "APACHE CHIEF," *Flying Higher: An Anthology of Superhero Poetry*, eds. Michael Damian Thomas and Shira Lipkin (2013).
Severson, Diane. "Orbit," *The Mystic Nebula*, July 12, 2013, mysticnebula.com/2013/07/12/orbit/#more-1380.
Simon, Marge. "Alien Interrogation," *Silver Blade Magazine* 17.
Simon, Marge. "Mary Shelley's Notebook," *Songs of Eretz*, December 2013, eretzsongs.blogspot.com/p/e-zine_4.html.
Sng, Christina. "Allegra," *Tales of the Talisman* 8.3, November 2013.
Sturner, Jason. "Faerystruck Down," *Tales of the Talisman* 9.1, Summer 2013.
Sykora, Anna. "From the Soil," *Chrome Baby*, Bairn 6, robindunn.com/bairn6.htm.
Theodoridou, Natalia. "Blackmare," *Ideomancer* 12.4, ideomancer.com/?p=2648.
Valente, Catherynne M. "A Great Clerk of Necromancy," *Apex Magazine* 50, apex-magazine.com/a-great-clerk-of-necromancy/.

Watkins, William John. "Indefensible Disclosures," *Asimov's Science Fiction*, April/May 2013.
Wheeler, Lesley. "My Translation Wouldn't Be the Same as Yours," *Avatar Review* 15, avatarreview.net/AV15/category/poetry/lesley-wheeler/.
Winter, Laurel. "Even Cowgirls Spread the News," *The Magazine of Speculative Poetry*, Fall 2013.
Worra, Bryan Thao. "Five Flavors," *Expanded Horizons*, December 2013, expandedhorizons.net/magazine/?page_id=3342.
Worra, Bryan Thao. "The Robo Sutra," *Expanded Horizons*, July 2013, expandedhorizons.net/magazine/?page_id=3239.
Wytovich, Stephanie. "Black Bird," *Hysteria: A Collection of Madness* (Raw Dog Screaming Press, 2013).
Wytovich, Stephanie. "Crazy," *Hysteria: A Collection of Madness* (Raw Dog Screaming Press, 2013).
Zinos-Amaro, Alvaro. "Re-Obsolete," *Star*Line* 36.4.

ABOUT THE RHYSLING AWARDS

A Brief Introduction, Adapted from *Star*Line* 12.5–6 (1989)

In January 1978, Suzette Haden Elgin founded the Science Fiction Poetry Association (SFPA), along with its two visible cornerstones: the association's newsletter, *Star*Line*, and the Rhysling Awards.

The newsletter cuts straight to Elgin's purpose for founding this organization, since it acts as a forum and networking tool for poets with the same persuasion: fantastic poetry, from a science fiction orientation to high fantasy works, from the macabre to straight science, and onward to associated mainstream poetry such as surrealism.

The nominees for each year's Rhysling Awards are selected by the membership of the Science Fiction Poetry Association. Each member is allowed to nominate one work in each of the two categories: "Best Short Poem" (1–49 lines) and "Best Long Poem" (50+ lines). All nominated works must have been first published during the calendar year preceding that in which the awards are being given. The Rhysling Awards are put to a final vote by the membership of SFPA using reprints of the nominated works presented in this voting tool, the *Rhysling Anthology*. The anthology allows the membership to easily review and consider all nominated works without the necessity of obtaining the diverse number of publications in which the nominated works first appeared. The *Rhysling Anthology* is also made available to anyone with an interest in this unique compilation of verse from some of the finest poets working in the field of speculative/science fiction/fantasy/horror poetry.

The winning works are regularly reprinted in the Nebula Awards Showcase published by the Science Fiction and Fantasy Writers of America and are considered in the science fiction/fantasy/horror/speculative field to be the equivalent in poetry of the awards given for prose work—achievement awards given to poets by the writing peers of their own field of literature.

Printing and distribution of *The Rhysling Anthology* are paid for by the SFPA. If you would like to contribute to the organization so that we may continue to produce this and other publications and fund the organization's efforts, please send a check, made out to the Science Fiction Poetry Association, to:

SFPA Treasurer
P.O. Box 907
Winchester, CA 92596

or donate online via PayPal to SFPATreasurer@gmail.com. Receipts will be provided upon request.

CONTENTS

v	Acknowledgments
viii	The Rhysling Awards: A Brief Introduction
xii	Editor's Note: Elizabeth R. McClellan, 2014 Rhysling Chair
xiii	President's Note: Bryan A. Dietrich, SFPA President
xiv	2014 Rhysling Award Winners

Short Poems First Published in 2013

1	Leslie J. Anderson, "The Captain Speaks"
1	F.J. Bergmann, "Nephology"
2	F.J. Bergmann, "What She Dreams Of"
3	Ruth Berman, "How Many"
4	Robert Borski, "Liar, Liar"
5	Bruce Boston, "Music of The Stars"
5	Shelly Bryant, "View from the Oort Cloud"
6	Rachael Bundock, "singing the plains"
6	Gwendolyn Clare, "The Narrow Hours"
7	G.O. Clark, "Climbing Up the Sky"
8	Carolyn Clink, untitled tanka
8	David Clink, "A City of Buried Rivers"
9	Jennifer Crow, "Why I Sold My Soul to the Storyteller"
10	Jane Crowley, "Triptych"
11	James S. Dorr, "The Specialist"
11	Peg Duthie, "The Bed I Haven't Made Yet"
12	Amal El-Mohtar, "Turning the Leaves"
12	Joshua Gage, untitled haiku
13	Adele Gardner, "Wheels"
13	Nancy Hightower, "A Virtuous Woman"
14	Russell Jones, "After the Moons"
15	Sally Rosen Kindred, "Sleeping Beauty Makes Dinner"
16	Andrew Kozma, "Pinocchio in the Toothpick Factory"
17	Geoffrey A. Landis, "Rivers"
18	Dennis M. Lane, "The Waiting"
18	B.J. Lee, "Don't Call Me a Fairy"
19	John C. Light, "Doppelgänger"
20	Sandra J. Lindow, "Topic of Cancer"
20	Darrell Lindsey, "Leaving Papa"
21	Helen Marshall, "Bluebeard's Wife"
21	Mary McMyne, "Irène Joliot-Curie"
22	Adrienne J. Odasso, "Ivy"

23	Adrienne J. Odasso, "Rigel"
23	Terrie Leigh Relf, "While on the evacuation shuttle"
24	S. Brackett Robertson, "Rhythm of Hoof and Cry"
24	James Frederick William Rowe, "The Bone Cutter's Lament"
26	Sofia Samatar, "APACHE CHIEF"
26	Diane Severson, "Orbit"
27	Marge Simon, "Alien Interrogation"
28	Jason Sturner, "Faerystruck Down"
29	Anna Sykora, "From the Soil"
29	Natalia Theodoridou, "Blackmare"
30	William John Watkins, "Indefensible Disclosures"
31	Lesley Wheeler, "My Translation Wouldn't Be The Same As Yours"
32	Laurel Winter, "Even Cowgirls Spread the News"
32	Stephanie M Wytovich, "Black Bird"
34	Alvaro Zinos-Amaro, "Re-Obsolete"

Long Poems First Published in 2013

35	Mike Allen, "Hungry Constellations"
40	Leslie J. Anderson, "Ponies and Rocketships"
42	Megan Arkenberg, "Songs at a Crossroads"
45	Jenny Blackford, "Hungry as Living Sorrow"
46	Leigh Blackmore, "The Last Dream"
47	Bruce Boston, "Living on the Leys"
49	Lisa M. Bradley, "Riveted"
51	Jennifer Clark, "Interim Problem Report 119V-0080"
52	Kendall Evans, "Into the Deep"
55	David C. Kopaska-Merkel & Kendall Evans, "The Bagel Shop Across the Street"
56	Robert Frazier, "The Girl Who Tipped Through Time …"
57	Robert Frazier, "Your Clone and You"
60	Adele Gardner, "Diana's Justice"
62	Ada Hoffmann, "The Siren of Mayberry Crescent"
64	Sally Rosen Kindred, "Gingerbread House: The Apron's Lot"
66	David C. Kopaska-Merkel, "Backwater"
68	Geoffrey A. Landis, "Across the Dark, the Pioneers"
69	Mary Soon Lee, "Interregnum"
71	Rose Lemberg, "I will show you a single treasure from the treasures of Shah Niyaz"
73	Sandra J. Lindow, "Timeline Tapestry"
75	Helen Marshall, "The Collected Postcards of Billy the Kid"
77	Jason Matthews, "Special Delivery from the Unnamed Quadrant"
79	Adrienne J. Odasso, "Heaven and Earth"
80	Dominik Parisien, "Sand Bags"
81	Qyn, "Ophelia"
82	Marge Simon, "Mary Shelley's Notebook"

84	Christina Sng, "Allegra"
85	Catherynne M. Valente, "A Great Clerk of Necromancy"
92	Bryan Thao Worra, "Five Flavors"
94	Bryan Thao Worra, "The Robo Sutra"
96	Stephanie M. Wytovich, "Crazy"
98	The Rhysling Award Winners 1978–2014
101	SFPA Grand Master Award Winners
102	How to Join the SFPA

EDITOR'S NOTE

Welcome to the 2014 *Rhysling Anthology*, in which you will find monsters and space and fairy tales and science and folklore and all manner of earthly delights. It is my sincere hope that you enjoy it, that what is in it represents to you the best that speculative poetry had to offer the world in 2013, and that you will so choose, if you are a voting member, to make your voice heard regarding which six of all these gorgeous poems are the best of the best.

Thanks to every one of the nominees under consideration, especially those who gave kind words, who gave assistance, who spoke with encouragement. Thanks to David Lee Summers for handling the publication end of matters and cover design, and to David Kopaska-Merkel for extending the invitation to be this year's Chair and providing his assistance throughout the process. Gratitudes beyond measure are extended to InDesign Wizard (Level 1) Christopher A. Johnson, who handled layout, and InDesign Wizard (Level: CLASSIFIED) and Associate Editor Ashley Brown, without whom this anthology would not exist. All failings herein are ultimately my own; all other errors are the fault of the bookbears.

My work on this year's anthology is dedicated to my grandmother, Doris Marie McClellan, who died before it could be published and who was so proud of me for being its editor. She had the very first *Rhysling Anthology* I ever appeared in in her copious collection of books and read it, even where she admittedly didn't understand some of it, with the same reverence for the literary arts that she instilled in me throughout her life. I miss her. She lives in song and story now—and in the words of speculative poet and mistress of the liminal arts S.J. Tucker, "storytellers never die."

Enjoy the poetry.

—Elizabeth R. McClellan
popelizbet@gmail.com

Elizabeth R. McClellan is a poet, editor, lawyer and occasional loudmouth who lives in the geographic center of the State of Tennessee and thus considers the whole state her backyard. She is a previous Rhysling Award nominee and winner of the Naked Girls Reading Literary Honors Award, and served as Articles Editor for Volume 42 of the *University of Memphis Law Review*. Her work has appeared in the *Moment of Change* and *I Know What I Saw* anthologies, as well as *Apex Magazine, Calliope Magazine, Goblin Fruit, The Legendary*, NewMyths.com, and *Stone Telling*. For more about Elizabeth, follow her on Twitter at @popelizbet, check out her author page on Facebook at tinyurl.com/ermcFB or visit elizabethrmcclellan.com.

PRESIDENT'S NOTE

Welcome to the *Rhysling Anthology*. We have encountered many challenges this year. This edition, the final one, is a variant which has been agreed upon by all editors and officers. Opinions vary, concerns oscillate, but the poetry found in these pages is eternal. Please enjoy the words of the authors celebrated herein. If you wish to see the first edition, it is archived on the SFPA website.

—Bryan A. Dietrich
kryptonnights@yahoo.com

NOTE: *A longer version of this Editor's Note appeared in the first print and e-publication editions of this anthology, addressing the Chair's criticisms of issues within the Science Fiction Poetry Association. Since these concerns were time-sensitive and primarily addressed to the SFPA membership, by mutual agreement with the President, the Editor's Note has been redacted, and the President's Note and Editor's Final Comment addressing the redacted matters do not appear in this edition. These materials may be accessed as they originally appeared at sfpoetry.com/files/2014RhyslingRedactions.pdf.*

2014 RHYSLING AWARD WINNERS

2014 Rhysling Award—Short Poem
"Turning the Leaves" by Amal El-Mohtar (p. 12)
First appeared in *Apex Magazine* December 2013

Amal El-Mohtar is the Nebula-nominated author of *The Honey Month*, a collection of poetry and prose written to the taste of twenty-eight different kinds of honey. Her work has appeared in several magazines and anthologies including *Uncanny, Lightspeed, Stone Telling, Apex, Mythic Delirium*, and *Strange Horizons*. Most recently her short fiction has appeared in *Lightspeed* magazine's Women Destroy Science Fiction special issue and *Kaleidoscope: Diverse YA Science Fiction and Fantasy Stories*. She is a founding member of the Banjo Apocalypse Crinoline Troubadours, edits *Goblin Fruit*, a quarterly journal of fantastical poetry, and lives in Glasgow with her fiancé and two jellicle cats.

2014 Rhysling Award—Long Poem
"Interregnum" by Mary Soon Lee (p. 69)
First appeared in *Star*Line* 36.4

Mary Soon Lee was born and raised in London, but became a naturalized US citizen in 2003. She has had over a hundred poems published, in places ranging from the *Atlanta Review* to *Star*Line* to the *Pittsburgh Post-Gazette*. Once upon a time, she also wrote short stories, including appearances in *The Year's Best SF* #5 and *The Year's Best Fantasy* #4. She is currently working on *The Sign of the Dragon*, an extended poetry sequence featuring dragons, demons, and a heroic king, a small part of which may be read at thesignofthedragon.com. She lives in Pittsburgh with her husband, two children, and two cats.

Second Place—Short Poem
"Rivers" by Geoffrey A. Landis (p. 17)
First appeared in *Asimov's Science Fiction* June 2013

Second Place—Long Poem
"Hungry Constellations" by Mike Allen (p. 35)
First appeared in *Goblin Fruit* Fall 2013

Third Place—Short Poem
"Music of the Stars" by Bruce Boston (p. 5)
First appeared in the 2013 *Balticon Program Book*

Third Place—Long Poem
"I will show you a single treasure from the treasures of Shah Nihaz" by Rose Lemberg (p. 71)
First appeared in *Goblin Fruit* Summer 2013

When I heard the learn'd astronomer,
When the proofs, the figures, were ranged in columns before me,
When I was shown the charts and diagrams, to add, divide, and measure them,
When I sitting heard the astronomer where he lectured with much applause in the lecture-room,
How soon unaccountable I became tired and sick,
Till rising and gliding out I wander'd off by myself,
In the mystical moist night-air, and from time to time,
Look'd up in perfect silence at the stars.

Walt Whitman, *Leaves of Grass*

SHORT POEMS FIRST PUBLISHED IN 2013

The Captain Speaks
Leslie J. Anderson

The computer reports the date and fills his glass.
It's the future, but he's too tired for it.
There were hardly any worlds
left to conquer, he moans. The computer
does not care. *I stabbed flags into empty deserts*
all my life. Then they were bulldozed, I guess.
Become a spaceman! they said. Adventure! Sex!
But no one says: oh, there aren't actually
any alien civilizations to battle, didn't we tell you?
No blue-scaled trollops to woo, or phosphorescent jaguars to shoot
with a heavy and beautiful laser gun. There is nothing
out here.

But once, some little thing
ran out of the sand. It was
clear and beautiful, like a ship of glass,
like a hermit crab—that size and
made of a million balanced pieces.
It was ornate. It was impossible.
I lowered my shaking pistol
and fired three shots into the ground
and it ran and ran ...

Nephology
F. J. Bergmann

Their atmosphere was thick, a bisque
of fog. They would not believe we came
from space; they held that nothing existed
beyond the omnipresent, lowering clouds
except heaven. To them, cankerous scars
and burnt oxides on the hull were proof:
our ship had come out of the molten core
of the planet, emerging from a volcano
or one of the bottomless magma abysses
prophesied to glow under the everlasting
polar nights. When we described *stars*,
their puzzled expressions were painful

for us to watch as they creakily unwound
their toroidal coils into open question
marks facing toward a blank gray ceiling,
the end of their world just overhead.

What She Dreams Of
F. J. Bergmann

> She dreams of it on special occasions. —james lee, "if"

Usually it decomposes quietly, mobster corpse
stashed under the brain's wet cement,
raccoon cadaver in the moonlight
on the potholed shoulder of the royal road,
heaving with maggots.

It thinks in maledictions. It hangs itself
in the closet and waits for her to come in.
Its head turns toward mirrors. Light moves away
from it quickly and pretends they've never met;
dark gets stuck inside it.

It obtained an advanced degree
from the School of the Americas,
where it always got extra credit. It hums
to itself frequently; off-key renditions of Puccini
or Led Zeppelin.

It used to give her ideas,
which she acted upon when the opportunity
presented itself, until something else told her to stop.
It wants to hide a weapon in one of her body cavities.
Be Preemptive is its motto.

It hates the medication
that keeps it silent, gag of wadding
ending in *zine* or *zone*. When it reanimates
and wades out of the flooded culvert of her nightmares,
it knows why it has been summoned.

How Many

Ruth Berman

How many —
Well, it depends.
Self expression,
Room for one's plenty.
Wings, by the way,
Give a real lift
To any grand jeté going.
Glory! sings the solitary dancer.

For mutual expression of esteem—
Also known as Love—
It has to have room for two.
Waltzes are especially mutual,
But some like fandangos
And some the turkey trot.
They're usually not quite up to date.

Mostly, though, it's a communal sort of thing,
The glory of the universe,
And you need eight at least,
And somewhere near a ninth to call:
Dive for the oyster!
Dig for the clam!
Not to mention, tenth,
Chagalling overhead
To make up the minyan,
The angel with the fiddle.

Reason you can never find pins
When you want them—
They're out in use.
Pinhead dancefloors ring
Too high for mortal ears
To notes that tell the angels:
Honor your partners!
Promenade home!

Liar, Liar

Robert Borski

Something is seriously wrong,
he must have misheard or misunderstood
Gepetto's casual remark to the guildmaster
about the little blue pill's
properties—"Talk about wood!"
Subsequently, the next time he lies,
his nose stays the same,
but *it* grows—what, in fact,
was barely a burl or nubbin
on the original piece of wood,
has already surpassed twig size,
swelling to a branch, then forking,
each tine now beginning to bear leaves,
the green acne of adolescence.

Even as birds with nest-building
materials invade and flit
about the workshop
all of the lady marionettes strike
their most provocative poses,
further embarrassing the boy,
who continues to deny snooping
amidst their crinolines.

No sapling now, he fears too
the growing pressure within,
the looming incontinence of phloem
and pine tar.

What to do, what to do? Furiously,
his wooden brain searches for solutions.

A last-ditch effort with the bellows
and a pit of coals appears promising
at first.

Alas, only his pants remain lit.

Moments later,
hearing his stepfather's footsteps
in the hallway,
reluctantly, the man-boy picks up a saw.

Music of the Stars
Bruce Boston

The music of the stars is
so very faint it is drowned
by the sounds of the city,

the steady drone of traffic,
the whine of sirens wailing
through day and night,

the clamor of crowds and
the hubbub of the media.
The music of the stars is

so very faint it is lost
in the static of the rain,
the timbres of the wind

batting against the trees,
in the rhythm of waves
consuming the shore.

The music of the stars is
so very faint, yet there
remain those of a certain

mind and heart who listen
hard enough to hear it,
never completely sure

what kind of music it is,
yet convinced it is the
one they must dance to.

View from the Oort Cloud
Shelly Bryant

a journey begun
the night he came home
to new locks, a new face
upon his pillow
traveling far enough to learn

the sun
need not be the brightest star

hoping
to find life of some sort
in another's glow

singing the plains
Rachael Bundock

she sings elephants to me as my eyes close
humpbacks rising from the river
whales of the plains; dried out
collapsing into their own wrinkles
with age, like her.
back to the river with me soon, she croons.
she remembers it before it happens—
her death.
passing into the water,
a baptism in reverse.
wrinkling elephants and
long-legged shell-birds,
slick scale brushes around her ankles.
and death,
a woman so beautiful
she can summon your soul from your body
by netting your eyes with hers.
rising from the riverbed—
legless and dripping deepmud brown,
hair knotting into a shroud.
black-ochre stripes passing over her skin
and mangrove swamps in her hair.
she sings elephants
and elephants sing back.

The Narrow Hours
Gwendolyn Clare

They call him Dreamer—he, who is always awake,
working through the slim and silent hours,
wedged between the last drunkard stumbling down a gaslit street
and the first weary farmer of the glistening predawn.
Working best in this final, brief respite of night,

he can sniff each sleeper's restless dream,
a taint of wakefulness lingering on the air, his patient air
tense like a waiting breath.

He unpacks his clockwork brain, links the gears just so,
winding the coiled spring with a practiced twist twist twist,
hands steady and quick, their motions automatic,
the flawed contradiction of his all-too-natural flesh and cold,
shining brass, denying him rest. So
he dons the watchmaker's loupe, night after night—
featherlight touch dancing across the delicate tools, he tinkers
with his imperfection.

He no longer recalls if he is the maker
or the made—the past mired in the strata of impossible
half-truths and half-believed deceits,
irrevocably lost in the well-polished labyrinth of his mind.
The claustrophobic press of day spawns
doubts to afflict him—unfit among the waking,
the only cures for his confusion are stillness
and the ready dark.

But in these narrow, infinite hours he knows
in his heart (one part still made of the old flesh) that
while some ways cannot be unwalked,
he will make a path forward
to perfection.

Climbing Up the Sky
G. O. Clark

Here's to all the
model rockets we blasted
towards the stars, always striving
to go higher, so many Saturday
afternoons dreamt away.

Here's to that first true
rocket ride, sixty-plus miles
straight up, a few minutes' wonder,
the freedom of weightlessness,
a boy's dream come true.

Here's to the star fighter
I earned my wings in, and

those mock battles with imaginary
aliens in the cluttered vacuum
of near Earth orbit.

Here's to the first
shuttle I ever co-piloted,
deemed obsolete by the powers that be,
parked in a dusty corner of some
crater on the Moon.

Here's to that old
freighter and mismatched crew,
asteroid dented, life times lamented,
ghost of my very first command,
rust-bucket retired.

Here's to my pride
and joy, *Tomorrow's Child*,
solar sail pleasure craft, panels aglow,
sixty five feet from stem to stern,
and the solitude of space.

And here's to the one-way
starship that I'm now captain of,
bound for some light-distant colonies,
a boy's dream become this
old man's final blessing.

[untitled]

Carolyn Clink

the winged serpent draco
slithers around polaris
circling—
a constellation
of leftover stars

A City of Buried Rivers

David Clink

You can hear it, the urgency of water.
It is 2:28 a.m. in the chronicle of the world's murmur.

You wait till you and the rivers are alone,
ask them how it feels to never stop,

how it felt when sky and cloud
disappeared into fluid memory.

Rivers begin with the tears of a giant tortoise
that finds its eggs broken, snake tracks in the sand.

You want to roll up the city in an Afghan carpet,
let the rivers bask in sunshine.

You see people you knew just below the blue's surface—
you grab them, shake them, yell *breathe* to their faces.

It is 2:32 a.m.
You can feel it, the urgency.

Why I Sold My Soul to the Storyteller
Jennifer Crow

His voice aches in my wing-sprung bones,
hollow and wishing for flight
out of the bondage of dreams.
A trick of the heart, that moment
of foolish hope, for I crave above all
a story no one else has heard
from his lips. Like a ghost
his whisper in my ear, and I know—
I think I know, I hope I know—
the weight of his gaze on bare skin
at the nape of my neck
as I bend my head to listen.
He will tell me of the visions I've forgotten
in the slow years of my captivity
and sing of worlds beyond this,
where green fields still stretch
like satisfied cats under the sun,
and true hearts once more
ride out against dragons. And he will promise,
promise me that my own tale
won't end here, listless patterns
carved in unwilling flesh.
Surely he knows the power
he holds on his tongue,

a tale, a tale for you, he says,
and I reach through gilded bars
because perhaps, this time,
I will know the words by heart.
And if this is hell, a snippet of story
glowing just out of reach,
at least it is my story, deep enough
to crack me open
and bare the knot of sorrows at my heart.

Triptych

Jane Crowley

What We Had

deer-hide kisses and blood in your teeth,
the thrill of the chase and stakes set steep,
certain death, and rebirth—
the promise of more than kind words
once you wake from feigned sleep.

Where You Are

kith and kin—enough, perhaps, save what you left
in the chapel-croft's green: love running deeper
than a boy-king's vows, fiercer than his icy queen.

How You'll Find Me

by the stones underfoot,
by the hoarfrost, and by
the harsh truth of prayers misspoken;
by the windblown scent of wine,
by light of the Plough as it crosses the sky.

The Specialist
James S. Dorr

"I think of it as a service," she said,
"like you know how global warming comes from an excess of carbon dioxide,
so anything that takes some of that away, like a tree maybe,
provides a service.
So there's medical problems too, you know,
like high blood pressure kills millions every day
and one would think a vampire, like me,
who goes out of her way to relieve those who suffer
by skimming off an occasional pint or two
should be thanked, not reviled.
Good God, you don't want to have people exploding right out on the street,
because, through neglect, their pressure got too high!
So think of us, rather, as Nature's safety valve,
not something to be killed with stakes or crosses,
or chased off with garlic.
That doesn't work with Italian vampires anyway, by the way.
But, as I say, think of me as your friend, not a monster to be destroyed,
rather a nurse-practitioner, as it were, as you extend your head forward for me,
in what one might call a specialized kind
of neck-acupuncture."

The Bed I Haven't Made Yet
Peg Duthie

Though I'm no princess, I'd let myself dream
that sleeping in mid-air would tame my hair.
To wake up with no need to soak or steam
my matted tresses, or to comb and swear
and comb some more—it would have been so sweet
to flaunt the mane of fairy-tales—to slide
from sleep still looking polished as a doll
and there's the rub. I am no Nancy Neat.

My feet forever track in what's outside;
my hair soaks up the winds. They take a toll
I wish I didn't mind having to pay.
I try to be sanguine, forbearing, mild
but Mama can't forgive my tomboy play—
her "can't you be a girl?"—it makes me wild.

Turning the Leaves
Amal El-Mohtar

These are the days of silver, and of gold—
the panting cold, the burst of bright on black
as coins sprout from trees, shiver, fall,
pave the streets with change.
Strange is the turn and tilt of day,
when stray, streaming, fingerling light
gleams slant against the eyes—the scold
of crows, magpies, jackdaws, gulls,
shouting the season in.
We count our birds. We read their wings. We script
stories in the scrim of puddled ice, tell tales
to ease the winter in. We sing
we had a lady, tall and fair
who spun the springing wheel for us,
who quenched our summer thirsts, who sank
her hands into the humid loam
and turned the understory. We had
a lady, warm and wise,
who bore us in her brimming arms,
who fed us all the very best
of fruit and root and flowered stem,
and if her blessing falls on us
we'll have her like again.
The wind is thin and grey, the sky
a half–drunk seeming—the gold will pale,
the silver streak and circuit into frost, the air
will spindle into needles—
but if her blessing falls on us,
we'll have her like again.

[untitled]
Joshua Gage

imagining
who this girl used to be
my trigger finger pauses.

Wheels

Adele Gardner

My lawn is filled by an ancient car.
I refuse to scrap it. I drive it,
My outlaw pleasure,
In the night, floating
Within its solid frame.

All day I feel its phantom wheel,
Turning like tilted wings at a feather's touch,
For the sky is blue as a Buick LeSabre,
Like a gull dancing alone above the highway …

What is dear to me is an albatross to others.
I scavenge gasoline from the junkyards—
Wrecks no one ever bothered to drain—
Like a graverobber feeding her pet zombie.
As dawn approaches, we slink home,
One long, smooth glide into base,
Mighty engine roaring joyfully
To warn the cats away from the wheels.

Early-bird neighbors stand on the corner
Waiting for the Lift to work,
Shouting complaints above my engine,
Their jealous eyes brushing the sleek lines of Big Blue
As it disappears through French doors into the rec room.
(Who has a garage these days?)
Their misty eyes and raucous chatter
Bring back the grind of their cars cranked onto the tow truck
One by one—crumpled in one rear-end tap,
Spluttering out-of-warranty to die in the drive,
Or permanently out of gas the morning after
The silent solar models seized the roads.

A Virtuous Woman

Nancy Hightower

my hands, rough and ruby-wrought,
the nails chipped and ragged,
can still grapple with your nightmares,
kneading them into poems.

i am the purple girl at market,
the crazy one with issues
of blood caking the underside. a sign
of stories to be told, my perfume
ready to be broken upon callused feet.

when i walk into circles, big as grendel,
the timing is always wrong.
i am heavy with weeping to be done,
warriors to be eaten, leaning into empty tomb,
asking where the gardener is.

despite all this, you can find me,
when dreams outhunt the wild caves
inside you, stick your heel
with poisoned arrows.
i'll throw poems into your eyes,
spit mud and water onto any wound
you please. we'll be healed the same
hour, legend has it, his word goes out.

After the Moons

Russell Jones

We came upon the plasma fields
accidentally. Our rockets burned
through the atoms of littered space, the dead.
We searched among the debris, hauled

their bodies on board. There were so many
we almost lost ourselves among them,
but in their radiation hardly recognised
the dimming lights they had become.

The scavenge order came, was carried out
smoothly. We burned the bodies, silent, roaring.
Through our windows their planets floated
like ice in a glass of bourbon. No morning

felt so dark in all that matter. We drifted
through the voids that angels could not
fill, rolled, shifted at the glances
of rock that hurtled past. We prayed, shot

photons into the deep emptiness.
What a strange grace. The captain broke
as he often did, his own dead world flooding
back to him. He played a recording

of a foghorn through the ship. Some decision
that was, billions of miles from any sea. In time
we settled by a lake of mercury, scattered
the remains, said our bon voyage. As we left

we saw natives cowered in knots, edging
to the mound of ash we'd left behind, bracing
as our thrusters brushed them outward. Our tools
were quiet once again in our safe darkness.

No lights flickered, the consoles lay lifeless.
And there was barely a word between us.
New moons were calling and we knew that
taking debris could be hazardous.

Sleeping Beauty Makes Dinner

Sally Rosen Kindred

I woke—cold kiss, that snow!—
I married you. And now
afternoon, I'm in your kitchen
bending through the tender heat,
tending what?—your black stove.
Today you hunt:
tonight you'll bring home
venison. Someone here
will baste the meat on a spit. I'm
your Briar Rose, your Beauty:
I'll do it, boil greens soft
as flesh, spear them with a fork
grief-keen as a spindle,
pepper them with my
sweat's pearls. I stir.
Or did I ever

wake? Would a Princess
be circling this pot,
her hand scarred from sleep's glass thorns
and feeling the push
of the dark ladle through the broth,

her hair rising to mist in its steam?
I love this heat. Is that right?
It's all too much like those years
of stained glass sleep, when dreams
finally named you: my hands
moving over the spoons
open and cold as your mouth
and the sound of your horse
beating back up the path,
the whinny's blue scrape
on the lips of the late, mistaken hour.

Pinocchio in the Toothpick Factory
Andrew Kozma

Sacrifice the cricket first. And then relax. They don't know
who you are or what tree you're born from. You've evolved,

just like your fellow workers, but from different stock. They talk
of malaria and syphilis, and you keep your wood-boring beetles

to yourself. But the floor manager has such strong, white teeth
you imagine him chewing oak to splinters. He smiles, and you smile,

and almost say you aren't afraid, but that would give you away.
Your nose would grow, and they would know. But console yourself,

little man, such teeth are rotting even as he speaks. His swampy breath
assaults your still-short nose, redolent of farts and death. He says,

"My boy, you're as reliable as a redwood, and as straight as an elm.
Oh, I like you, I do." Truthfully, you suspect he suspects.

Your sap runs cold. The only place that would hire you,
Geppetto said, though he had to fib a little on the forms. Oh God!

Oh father! Oh Geppetto! Is this what you'd planned for me?
They'll keep me lying here forever and never need another tree.

Rivers

Geoffrey A. Landis

```
In the darkness,                              Inside us,
   a luminous                              surrounding
      torrent:                             us: the
         the great                         river
            sky river                      of life
               a hundred                      branching,
                  billion stars                  flowing
                  We are                            through
               stranded on                         our veins
            a lonely                               from
         island                                 generation
      marked by                                to
   dust lanes                                generation
      a turbulent                        Warm, salty
         whirlpool                       ebbing
            moving                       and
               inexorably                   cresting from
                  through spaces              heartbeat to
                     too vast                    heartbeat,
                        for                      surging
                     comprehension            inexorably,
                  flowing too                 flowing to an
               slowly for                  invisible
                  mortal eyes              sea.
               to see.
            Before us,
               behind us:
                  the river
                     of time
                  We long
                     to gaze
                        beyond
                           the bend
                        to that
                     cataract
                     that we
                        can hear
                           in the
                              distance
                           We are
                              caught
                                 in the rapids,
                              borne downstream
                           rushing inexorably
                     to the future we will never see
```

The Waiting
Dennis M. Lane

I stand before the shrine, enamoured, surrounded by my bold breath
You, an ancient rock beneath a crystal shroud, with not one cold breath

Purple down cloaking your angels wings, the bed upon which you lay,
have lain since your fall to Earth, when you spent that last cruelly sold breath

My heart beats, calls out to you, my Goddess, but your breast does not stir
Each day I entreat you to return, but I see no cajoled breath

Those who remain outside the walls would strike me down if they but knew
that I watch, and wait, praying to you, hoping for that foretold breath

Lost souls that merely exist in the darkness that enfolds the land
They do not know your beauty, and would fear the touch of age-old breath

Ruby eyes, precious jewels to some, source—I pray—of loving glances
Yet still you lie unmoving, ignoring my cries you withhold breath

As I grow old my limbs stiffen, becoming the stone that I love
I, named the Archivist at my birth, await that first controlled breath.

Don't Call Me a Fairy
B.J. Lee

Don't call me a fairy
though I may be fae.
Watch over your child
lest I take her away.
I want to trade places
and live in your world;
grow up dressed in satin,
be prettily pearled.
I'll make the change quickly.
Don't worry: your gain!
Your real child will flourish
in wind and in rain,
out in the woods
with the best faery folk.
No, I'm not kidding.
This isn't a joke.

Don't call me a faery;
a real child I'll be.
We'll see if you notice
when your child is me.

Doppelgänger

John C. Light

Entering the lonely house with my wife
I saw him for the first time
peering furtively from behind a bush,
blackness that moved,
a shape amidst the shadows,
a momentary glimpse of gleaming eyes
revealed in the ragged moon light.
A closer look (he seemed to turn) might have
put him to flight forever.
I did not dare
for reasons that I failed to understand
though I knew I should act at once,
I puzzled over him, hiding alone,
watching my wife as she neared the gate,
he came and I saw him crouching,
night after night.

Night after night
he came and I saw him crouching,
watching my wife as she neared the gate.
I puzzled over him, hiding alone,
though I knew I should act at once,
for reasons that I failed to understand
I did not dare
put him to flight forever.
A closer look (he seemed to turn) might have
revealed in the ragged moon light
a momentary glimpse of gleaming eyes,
a shape amidst the shadows,
blackness that moved.
Peering furtively from behind a bush,
I saw him for the first time
entering the lonely house with my wife.

Topic of Cancer

Sandra J. Lindow

In the heat of midsummer,
my garden is eaten
as I am eaten.
tomatoes and zucchini halved,
cancer blooming in my left breast
like a lumpy, toxic rose.
After the mastectomy,
I am Amazonned
and ready for more battle:
the varmints must go.
A live trap set near the tomatoes
snares an angry woodchuck
and later an unhappy opossum.
Outside of town each is let go,
but cancer is never that easy.
In the heat of the hottest summer on record
I eat well, gearing for war.

Leaving Papa

Darrell Lindsey

Something in the gaze of ten thousand blackbirds
lays the mighty forest bare,
& the woodsman cannot even remember
the names of his children
who are running towards the nearest road
with thorns in their hands.
They shout in a broken tongue,
sense that time is either unwinding
or trying to reinvent itself.
They hear their late mother's voice
amid the heat shimmer,
& the woman who never drove
breaks the speed limit
right through the horizon.

Bluebeard's Wife

Helen Marshall

This is where I bury those beautiful young boys
with arms brown as cigar paper, their eyes a struck match.

I shall catalogue, if you wish, my dead lovers.
I keep their hearts in a jar of dull glass.

Here is a knuckle dark as olive wood,
a scapula, smoothed and scraped clean.

Here is the way to my bloody chamber
where disaster is a love song on the radio.

The door to my lesser sins I keep unlocked ,
and the door to my greater sins.

There is a place for you in my bone garden
but perhaps you will plant love in my heart.

Perhaps you will fill me all to bursting.

Irène Joliot-Curie

Mary McMyne

As a girl I learned the elements.
With a pencil my mother Marie
sketched the shapes of compounds:
the honeycomb of water, the zigzag
of sugar, the gridiron of salt.
This is the way it is, she said.
Everything has its own form.

I believed her until the day
I saw the woman in the mirror,
wide-hipped, lips as pink as a rose *paczek*.
Hair like water, as black as Roussin's salt.
Through alchemy of time,
I'd been transformed.

After that, I walked among men
and tasted their salt. I sampled
the sugar of their flesh, and wet lips.

After Frédéric and I—oh happy aggregate—
I was not prepared for the way it swelled my belly.
I was not prepared for the way it muddled my thought.

In the laboratory, we realized
the alchemist's sweet dream
of turning one element into another.
We turned boron into unstable nitrogen.
We turned alum into phosphorus
that wept and turned to salt.

Now, in this hospital named for my mother,
it is not the X-rays that possess me, not the saline,
the sugar-water, or the changes in my blood.
It is those first few months with Hélène,
all those nights I spent alone and not
at the lab window, transformed.

In this hospital bed, as the white room
breathes and flares into nonsense,
I keep falling back into the first night
I felt her inside me, her passage
from *nothing* into *something*
lighting mine into the dark.

Ivy

Adrienne J. Odasso

One fine morning, it's the ivy
that will show you: your bones
have all split at the seams. Arrows
are made easily from these. Learn
that nobody else has your back. Trust
is more often than not for the weak,
and love unforgivable. Your stone heart,
you must split in four; poison the quarters
with marrow from each shaft. It'll hurt
no greater than what wounds you have.
Always watch the ivy. Study both cracks
and rebinding. Nock swiftly now, aim quick
to court the kill. Your tendril-bound breath
fills each fissure like ivy. Now, watch.

Rigel

Adrienne J. Odasso

For Jane Yolen

I was fresh home from naming quasars
the night we first met, your silk-soft paws
pressed flush to my palms. Your eyes
were mismatched: one the color of bluets
stripped back; the other, new spring grass.

My grandfather taught me to hunt. He said
you'd prove a rabbit-chaser's friend, but my heart
and yours, dear girl, were set on a different prize—
dusk-wise, we wandered those rocky hillsides
in search of blue stars. You trained so swift
to the slightest turn of my hand, read warning
in the faintest puff of my wondering breath.

I'm glad now that I knew you in winter,
wolf-sister. Your first daughter would have run
with me had you not gone, might've greeted Orion
as a seasoned old friend. As I still do, my sweet,
and as I dream. As roaming we always did.

While on the evacuation shuttle

Terrie Leigh Relf

I rub my temples, murmur, "barometric pressure,"
to no one in particular, more to break the silence
that weighs heavier than gravity's absence, but
the woman strapped in next to me says, "No, honey,
it's the lack of oxygen going to your brain,"
and while I think her assessment doubtful,
I nod pleasantly (manners are even more
important where we're going), listen to her ramble
about oxygen deprivation and altered states
of consciousness while staring out the viewport
at the starless night, the looming insectoid structure
soon to be our home, while trying not to succumb
to yet another migraine or vomit up my daily rations
or worry about all those people who didn't make
the final shuttles, while pondering the sound of
ice caps melting, floodwaters rising, ten billion
stars embracing us before dawn.

Rhythm of Hoof and Cry
S. Brackett Robertson

She didn't worry at the first appearance of the horns,
small buds, nearly flush with his skull.
She assumed all men must grow them, when they're thirty
She'd forgotten he was human.

He was less certain about them, peaking above the crown of his head
but he was in her country now,
living behind the wall of thorns.
He'd been cut and bruised when he crossed, but that was a year ago.

He didn't tell her of his dreams, of the cold air and the restless bodies
and the urge to flee
he didn't tell her about the hounds.
He was afraid, when he awoke, but he told himself these things
      are usual here

Once they grew longer, started to show at the top of his shadow,
      she wondered,
quietly, how he was adjusting. The air was different here, and the water
he'd never drunk it before for fear of entrapment.
He said he was still, said he was calm, but he crossed the brambles
She'd seen his cuts. She'd seen the fear in his eyes when he awoke.

She heard the hounds when he rose from his bed,
moonlight gleaming on his horns, now reaching curved to the moon
when he looked towards her, it was with emptied eyes,
he startled when she reached towards him, and fled.

The Bone Cutter's Lament
James Frederick William Rowe

When I begin
I know that I
Must discard
More than God has taken
That they might walk
My saw shall cut
Inches higher than the wound
That muscle and flesh
    (This too must I waste)
    (And regret the loss of healthy flesh I do)

Might unnaturally join
Over cruelly shortened limbs
And form a stump
A useless end that has yet a use
To stabilize a peg

The war has taken many lives
But far more limbs are daily cut
And of these limbs
I know for each
How much excess bone is lost
Inches of bone
Bone which men beg me not to touch
And for which they cry when I remove
    (Their agony I sympathize)
    (But cut I must for their own good)
As they thrash and screech
And implore divine intervention
But God has already given unto me
Dispensation for this waste
This waste of precious bone

Allow me now to muse
Upon a subject most macabre
How many men have I wasted
In the bone I have removed?
I mean to say their skeleton
What weight in bone have I attained?
Is it enough to fill a man?
I dare say that it is more
    (Far more indeed I reckon)
    (Oh what misery it is to know!)
My surgeon stink I offer as proof
It follows me far beyond the table
And shall not be washed away
No, not so easily discarded
So unlike the bone

    I am the bone cutter
    And such is my lament.

APACHE CHIEF
Sofia Samatar

He grows. You have a big job he'll do it. APACHE CHIEF! In the comics he says *Inuk chuk*, we think it means *Big Man*, but in the show we just hear his name. We're eight, ten years old. We're never Apache Chief when we play, he's no fun, he can't talk right, what's the point of being big if nobody listens to you. APACHE CHIEF! His voice booms, he fills up the sky. Bigger doesn't always mean stronger. Our uncle is bigger than us but he can't talk right, he sleeps on our couch. Still learning English. You have a big job he'll do it. Apache Chief always stands in the background, because if he stepped in front, you'd never see anyone else.

Orbit
Diane Severson

Home has always had the comfortable pull of gravity.
When I was small I ran in circles
From Living Room through Dining Room
To Kitchen and on again.
The origin of my flight and orbit.
Observe the lumps to prove my bumpy take-off.
Home was a welcome constant—
The point from which my outward spiral began.
The tap, tap, tapping of her typing
And the tinkling of her piano playing
Was a comfort as I drifted off
To sleep preparing for what came next.
With lift-off came revolutions
Around town and then country.
Even traversing the water
Could not sever or break
The tether, proving it robust.
The pull of Home was steady
And so required the occasional return
Of the prodigal daughter.
I was not long enough in any one place
To call another Home.

She is letting go of the house now.
A heaviness of loss
Is jumbled with a lightness
Of being cut loose.
Where will Home be now?

She is free now to reposition
Her own orbit around my big, beloved brother
Whose own focal point shifted long ago,
He is warm and welcoming.
But my new trajectory,
Is a sudden, unfamiliar straight line,
I'm flung outward and away.
Where will it lead?
What new center will be found?
Will its pull of gravity be strong enough?
I hold still and open my senses, hoping I might
Hear that tapping, that tinkling.
But I realize what I'm hearing
Is a pitter-pattering and
My apprehension is relieved.
I've found an axis to revolve around.
And as I spiral in once more
I settle into its enveloping gravitation
And find I'm settling in around
Myself, my family. Home at last.

Alien Interrogation

Marge Simon

We place the chair in the white room
It is a plain chair, made of wood.
The floor is bare cement, stained.

The human is dragged into the room.
We place him upright in the chair,
securing him with chains.

Beethoven's *Third Symphony* begins,
telescoping diverse functions that occur
in rapid succession, a clash of discords.

A window appears beside him, revealing
a rainbow above a lush green forest.
Fey creatures emerge from the trees.
They have huge eyes and fragile yellow wings
that beat so rapidly they blur.
They hover at the window.

The human writhes in his bonds,
begins to cry. We shutter the window;

abruptly silence Beethoven.
We unchain him, help him to the door.

Beyond the door another window.
An alluring woman dances behind the glass.
Forest creatures swirl around her,
their bites leave angry welts on her arms and legs.
She never stops dancing to brush them off.

My assistant asks if we should take
the human to another room for further
observation, but I shake my head.

I remove the beautiful linen handkerchief
from the holster at my hip.
Ever so gently, I wipe away his tears.

Faerystruck Down
Jason Sturner

In the rolling fog of the purple sea
Where slugs infest the ridge
    And breeze-bent heather
      Tethers ghosts of the drowned

Beyond the threshold of the mind
Where sea hags howl at the moon
    And shapes unseen
      Sneak away human babes

Lies the maritime trail I was warned not walk
Urged by patrons of the old pub
To return to America, and be gone at next breath:
    "For too tempting is the tourist from afar!"

But I split my sides at their heathen pleas
Doused their cares with whiskey and ale
Till after a spell, I was cheered out of town
    Pushed along streets of leaping whispers

So onward to accursed shores I went
Bold with humor and the prod of drink
    Where fish-lipped merrows in cohuleen druiths
      Leered from frothy kelp isles

And the mutterings in belch-bogs grew ever near ...
And the perverted, creeping shadows ...

I will never forget their dream-drenched faces
As they sang and danced and picked over my end
Their goblets high in the salty spray of the purple sea
    Where many a mortal bone now rests in the deep

And in my last moments of earthly acquaintance,
Head a pivot and lit with fires green,
They branded my soul to the tongue of lore
    Forever to break out madly from seaside lips

From the Soil
Anna Sykora

Our tribe, which hoarded guns and tins,
Has slaughtered the wild ones for their sins
And raised up a beacon bright as gold;
Now only *our* stories can be told.

But sometimes out on patrol at twilight
I hear a humming from the soil;
I hear the songs that accuse us still,
And how they vow they always will.

Blackmare
Natalia Theodoridou

"Melanippe is a horse of a woman," the men say, joking among themselves,
because there is no word for
what Melanippe is.
"When you fuck Melanippe she neighs like a mare," they say.
"She's bloody dangerous too," they add and laugh. "Kicks like a horse."
"Her hoofs have broken men in half,
cracked their skulls into a million pieces."
And yet they come,
keep coming,
and Melanippe keeps kicking and cracking.

Melanippe trots by herself in her empty apartment.
"My Father Was Chiron the Centaur," she says, stressing every

first syllable in hopes of making it sound right,
"And I Am Melanippe the"
—but there is no word for female Centaurs—
"Centauress? Centauride?" she twists her tongue and neighs
and she trots back and forth in her apartment,
"Me.La.Nip.Pe," she says, stressing every syllable now,
every letter
every breath
it all comes out wrong no matter how.
"Horsewoman," she says, but it sounds more like "hoarsewoman"
or "coarsewoman"
and then words collapse in on themselves in the space around her,
and the room is filled with pointless things that simply won't do,
like *chairbed*, no good for sitting or sleeping, not for her;
and *blackmare*, that vision of herself which visits her sometimes, its legs
divided by two;
and *everstill*,
which is the word to describe the invisible motion of a stillborn babe.

Melanippe tries out this new language of hers:
"In my blackmare last night I saw the everstill creature slip from its
chairbed," she says,
and for a moment her heart catches on something,
but then the words fall flat
on the floor in front of her hoofed feet
and break into a million pieces.

She studies them, uncertain.
They look a bit like men's skulls,
don't they? she thinks as she picks them up,
one by one,
and one by one she lets them drop again.

Indefensible Disclosures

William John Watkins

The Federal Center for Controlling Things
wishes to know where I contracted poetry,
so those infected, or at risk, can be advised.
They have a list of everything that sings,
and since my name appears on two or three
of their cross-referenced indices, I am apprised
that I have been identified as dangerous
to the well-being of my contacts, who must be disclosed
to the bureaucracy in charge of my disease.

They warn me my condition's serious,
and often leads to suicide in those disposed
to introspection and the vague unease
that poets, on the whole, spread like a pestilence
among the uninfected and naive
who think a truth innocuous because it rhymes.
Contamination is a grave offense
and I am given to believe
that, though my malady is no crime,
I still am subject to grave penalties
if I withhold the names of those from whom I got,
or those to whom I gave, this metaphoric flu,
and since I'm not the hero that I ought to be,
and though I know it's something you would never do,
I write this poem leading them to you.

My Translation Wouldn't Be the Same as Yours
Lesley Wheeler

Since you feel cheated, having missed the pie,
here's what I heard. The slither of a shotglass
on a homemade board. Jangle of a clock
shaped like a rooster. Children mouth-breathing
as their mothers practiced the art of prying questions.
Sugar crusting hard beneath our nails.
When the French doors shook, *bam bam bam*,
as if a big dog begged on his hind legs
for us to open up, we shrieked and fled.
The eldest boy remained to look, as in every
children's book, but nothing was there. No reason.

Remember chasing the ice cream truck, its frozen
chime glinting at the corner, too far to catch?
Imagine it rushes at you, roaring, *Wake up.*
Be kind. Slow down. Keep your head clear. It's not
about you, but you are important. Taste it all.
It's hard to wait with silver on your palm.

The next afternoon, Ouija pizza box
recycled, my sister warmed her casseroles
while I played Trouble with my nephew. The baby
kept seizing the pegs, yelling, *My turn now.*
At last I stepped through the latticed doors, their sheers
rigid and bright, onto the cold back deck.
You could see the whole development sloping

to a marsh where some trees survived. Large houses
on lots fenced identically in vinyl.
Stupid to scare the kids like that. If
you're brave enough to wonder, show them you're brave
enough for answers, to maintain intention:
not to have listened, but to listen always.
A pitifully belated will to pay
attention, undo the lock, and call *yes please*.

Even Cowgirls Spread the News
Laurel Winter

The buzz transports me back
from postmodern hoohah
and some skinny old cowboy
—'bout forty, no spring chicken in 1868—
sputters water out his nose
and drops his canteen.
I admit I'm quite the scene
in a latex bikini and belly button ring.
Too bad for him I have to make him forget me.
Too bad for me I'm buzzed into this time period
—and this effing corset—until 1873.
Time enough to turn heads
and turn myself into a school marm
and turn a few ideas upside down.
I say time is an omelette
and I've never been afraid of breaking eggs.

Black Bird
Stephanie M. Wytovich

I ask of you,
Can a dead soul cry?
Can it weep tears of blood
As it wails in the shadows
Of lost loves and empty bottles?
Can it mourn the memories
Of abandonment and neglect,
Sew up the prideful wounds
Of ink-spattered rejection,
Cast out in the dust-covered
Compositions no one got to read?

I ask of you,
Can a heart still hurt
After it's stopped beating?
Does pain fade into the ether
Of dusk into dawn while
Ravens sing their funeral songs
Over his rose-laden grave?
Do they mock him in unison?
Squawking at the man who
Died for his art, whose words
Wove madness into a definition
Of sanity? Whose stories bled
Out like a Tell-Tale Heart,
Whose metaphors tapped
At our doors, relentlessly
Questioning our reason,
Our judgment, our sobriety?
Nevermore!

I ask of you,
Does the damned fear
The shape of death?
Does it cringe at the fluttering
Blackness that hangs over its head
Like a dark cloud in the blue sky?
Does the winged beast unsettle
Even the deadliest of creatures?
A marauder even to the master
That brought it to life? Does the
Raven speak blasphemy, rhyming
With a serpents tongue, eyes gleaming,
Like a 'demon that is dreaming'?
Can it see into our souls?

I ask of you,
Does the feather of the
Black bird bring the reaper?
Arms open, scythe extended,
No more questions,
Nevermore!

Re-Obsolete

Alvaro Zinos-Amaro

If the rose is obsolete,
then by any other name
it is obsolete too.

When Armageddon arrives,
a gift will be made
of thunder, and roses,
and sweet green grass;
even if these things cannot last.

And, after the fires,
when the fragility of the flower
has been restored,
there will come soft rains,
and once again
it shall become obsolete.

LONG POEMS FIRST PUBLISHED IN 2013

Hungry Constellations
Mike Allen

Prologue: Possibilities

Like the giants who boil under the land,
whose broken baby teeth form mountains,
or their sisters who seethe unbearable heat
in crevasses beneath the sea,
stars burn with appetite,
huge and slow,
diffused and directed through the legends
that pin them in place.

Another cosmos, a mere crêpe layer away,
shall afford us the best seats in the house.
Peel aside the sweet starch of time and distance and step through. Here
the night sky's the stage once
the curtain of day rises.
Celestial bodies array themselves at impossible speeds,
acting out their stories in real-time for a globe-spanning audience.

The peoples here watch from their chateau skylights,
from their glassine-flimsy city domes,
from broad ships like wooden continents,
from arid plain and barren rock and glacier palaces.
Even the fey, real as you or I,
herd their captives out to catch the show,
the scattered soup of night become platform and proscenium.

How these incendiary orbs
hunger for our observation, our admiration,
the power of the human eye to enliven what's devoid.
With ardor they devour the scripts we dream for them,
then improvise.

Constellations shift before our eyes,
their tales our tides.
Their shadows our losses.
Their orbits our lies.
The Fox Smiled, Famished

Gather around.

Gather around the largest fire of all,
large enough to warm the lands
on the other side of the world,
to brighten all your moons.

My burning coat swells redder by the day.
My teeth are curls of flame, my tail a flare.
My tale? Come closer. Hear it.
Closer still—the ending is a secret.
Each of you will hear
as I whisper in your ear.
Other planets joined this circle before yours, yes.
I cannot fathom where they've gone.
Come closer yet and I'll share my guess.
You're practically standing on my nose,
basking in my boiling breath.

Let me pick you up, little world,
little pup in my jaws.

The Serpent Is Tempted

It's a principle of the universe
that everything spirals
to an intimate squeeze—
the sinuous limbs of galaxies,
the crush of gravity.

I have no fruits for you to pluck—
they shine so far away, so hot,
how could you reach?
How could you bite?—
it's *your* hidden warmth,
your blood-salt oceans,
the scattered lights of your
night-time habitats like
so many wide-eyed mice,
that call to *me*.

Dim stars demarcate my spine,
winding side to side
as I slide to you.

How I long
to flicker subtleties
before your eyes,
twin comet tails

joined in a forked tongue.
How I long
to thaw
against your molten heart.

The Spider Sends Gifts

The event horizon
bounds the edge of my web.
Your scholars claim nothing can emerge from my silk,
no morsels that alight within, not even
my own burnt-cinder body.
Shine the spotlight here, you'll see nothing,
maddening absence,
and even more troubling hints of motion
as the sleek, dark arches of my legs
quiver at frequencies undetectable
by eye alone.

Then,
the milkweed spill scatters from my funnel,
wriggling specks of stardust drifting,
spinning light,
Doppler strands lengthening behind,
firework sparks burning brighter as they
crawl to you—
all my hundred thousand babies,
hunting for new homes.

The Crow Migrates from the Outer Dark

Alone among the cosmic menagerie, I am defined
not by bones drawn in stars but by black between;
as my wings eclipse, their desperate shine
bends around my feathertips, begging for your gaze.

To you, lovely worms, I'm but a lone eye
staring back at you on deepest nights
when your fires gutter out and the turbines
that charge your cities falter.

So far away you still haven't noticed
how each year my single star glows brighter,
plunging inward at the speed of light.

The curve of my wings once marked
the rim of the universe.

They still do,
that boundary shrinking
with my eons-long dive.

When I arrive, your sons and daughters
countless generations hence—those who survived
the fox's snapping jest, the thousand spider nests,
the serpent's airless smother—will see naught
in their sky but the emptiness inked in my quills,
the scavenging void's sharp beak.

Interlude: Truth

The truth, some claim, has a portrait of its own
riddled through the Cosmic Sphere's black shell
that admits its deep blue light,
refraction of an unseen power.

The fey pestilence who in this layer of what can be
hold sway in forest mounds and mountain hearts
claim these pinpricks of azure
are not stars, but tunnels outside time,
the heads of the trails they followed, that ended here.

Yet what shape do these mysteries take in this sky?
Some claim a lyre, longing for fingers
to coax songs of grief and war.
Some claim a balance, its empty scale
fed human hearts found wanting.
Some claim a veil, which hides a face
that aches for our regard, its beauty
sure to blind all beholders.

The Hunter Takes Aim

So many villains fill this sphere with their lanterns.
My own stars dance to sketch a bow, draw back
to manifest an arrow.

The boys among you cheer
to see me rise broad-shouldered,
my breastplate stained with pale blood of nebulae,
my belt clustered with glowing hides.

The wise among you wonder
whose skins hang flayed
when predatory stares populate the sky

from horizon to zenith.
Do they dare wonder aloud?

In your lands squat my temples
of marble and topaz, almost beautiful
as the square-jawed, cleft-chinned,
sharp-cheekboned face
enshrined within—
the effigy you've masked me in,
exquisite and unblinking.
Millions kneel before my gaze
and avert their eyes.

No wastelands more hostile exist
than the surfaces of stars and
the gulfs they sail.
Question what allegiances I've made to survive
and my faithful will find you,
their aim as sure as mine.

The Prince Tightens His Embrace

My jeweled arms join, a glittering circle.
All that's wed to me sealed between them.
All you will bear for me stays crushed
close to my heart. I force your orbits
smaller and smaller. My fury grows
each time you try to move. When I die of rage
the burst will tear you atom from atom.

The Dragon Shields Her Young

I am

a river of stars and scales and fire and milk and all the things that thrive in the alchemical reactions where they meet.

I am

my own soul and all the others too, every single constellation in the sky. Not one of them can stop the chimerical redactions as I claim their shapes, their minds. I do this at will, but they can never in return claim mine.

The gale of my flight strips the fox's fiery hide. My coils ensnare the serpent, braid him, make him poison his own tail.

My mouth gapes to scoop the spider's brood, Leviathan straining krill,
their dying embers tickling my throat.

My gulf-spanning shriek scares the crow back to the rim of time. My
claws snap the hunter's arrow and my teeth drive him back into the day.

A single strike, the ring of the prince's arms severed at the wrists.

All of you

watch as it ends, as my own curtain descends, as I add your blue bauble
to my hoard, warm you against my belly, my sleeping egg.

Epilogue: Lies

In the end they're all consumed,
just as you and I, in that world or our own
are fodder for the heartless sun
that crushes all with chariot wheels,
its dream-slaying curtain drug behind
to show us our true predators
are close at hand, close as our hands,
as the blocking we follow on this slum-rot stage
when our gazes cannot fix upon the stars—
we play our parts
and pray our strands of plot won't end
until the night begins again,
the tales resume.

Ponies and Rocketships
Leslie J. Anderson

Ponies and rocketships are the blackest of magic
because they exist in your mind beyond sin and debt,
a heroic nirvana of open ranges and deep space.

Because as little girls and little boys we believed we could have them
and we ran around the house with our fingers like ray guns
and our pink cowboy hats long before we understood
the complex historical and social ramifications
that made our dreams impossible.

Also that people shoot mustangs now because they trample vegetables,
and light speed travel hasn't even been invented yet.
They probably believed in ponies and rocketships once too.

Ponies and Rocketships are horrible things
because we have always watched movies
that tell us heroes ride ponies and rocketships
into suns, and we fell for it every time
and still hope we
will ride into suns and sunsets.

And one day you realize it's impossible,
and also you will not be president.

My mother wished for them for every Christmas
and ran out in the snow in her bare feet
while her mother called her an idiot
from the kitchen window in her bare feet.

And she threw open the garage door and found
only her parents' VW van and the little puddle of oil—
the old rusted tools that she would leave
for years after her father died.
She never found a pony or a rocketship
and neither will you.

What will actually happen is something like this:
you will get into the college of your choice, that you can't afford,
and the poet goddess of your department will call you practical
as if it's a contagious disease, and you will feel
like you have become a minor character.
You will find an uncomfortable peace in this and you will get very drunk
very often.
You will wake up next to people. You will walk
down dark alleys and get in at least one fist fight.
You will smash your head against the ground
and feel very strange for a day, but refuse
to go to a hospital. You'll be fine.

You will work much longer than you are being paid for.
You will be praised for your determination or not.
And you will play by the rules and still
not find a job to pay the money you owe and you will
wonder why you ever wanted to go to space
or chase outlaws in the first place.

You will wonder
what kind of debt *that* would have gotten you.

And then you might meet someone
and lie on the floor eating popcorn

because you can't afford a couch yet
and talk about a time when you will afford
so many couches.

You crush out the tiny fleas
and talk of a time when you won't
wage a tiny war across your carpet.

Yes, Ponies and Rocketships are the darkest of magic, because
the fantasy will creep back into your life
no matter how practical you are
or how little wine you drink
or how few times in your life
you allow yourself to use the word *yeehaw*.

You will start thinking
of fighting space aliens again, maybe
only driving home from work, at stoplights,
or pouring eggs into a saucepan, but you will
think of them again.

You will plan what you would do
if someone galloped into your living room,
stuck out their hand and said,
There's no time!

If you are lucky—if you have lived your life well—
you will think of the movies and the day dreams,
the hopes and disappointments with a surprised affection—
a nostalgia like that for your first shitty car
or ratty apartment—

as if you were the hero,
as if these were your war stories
and they are.

Songs at a Crossroads
Megan Arkenberg

I.
Traveler, your only choice is what to lose;
This path will take your soul, this one your pride.
The choice is yours. I will not help you choose.

That snowy northern path—who could refuse
its ice-trapped loveliness, though death's implied
on such a road, and life is much to lose?

That southern trail in fiery autumn hues
would burn your mind to ash without a guide—
don't ask me. I'm not here to help you choose.

And east, a dragon's shadow makes a bruise
upon the yellow marshes where wyrms hide
their gold. Who can say what all you might lose

if you continue west beneath the yews
that whisper with the voice of one who died
while lost? I am not here to help you choose

your fate—although I wonder, sometimes, whose
face you picture, whose words help you decide
which limb, which year of life, which love to lose.
Or stay with me. I will not make you choose.

II.
South to the meadow, north to the field
or east to the sand rolling down to the sea?
O where, o where can this wound be healed?
O where is the home that waits for me?

North flies the gryphon, east rolls the foam,
and south roars the dragon to taunt the brave
but westward lies the road back home
and my lover in his shallow grave.

East brings glory, south gives treasure,
north spreads a feast with a noble host
but home is a prize beyond all measure
and west lies the man who loved me most.

III.
What is the price of your soul, O Traveler?
For what will you sign the Devil's book?
Stand at the crossroads, name your bargain.
A dead man raised? A furtive look

into the future that dangles before you,
twisting like a golden thread?
Your father's secrets? Your mother's knowledge?
A word in the tomb with the unhallowed dead?

The names of all beasts? The speech of dragons?
The wisdom bound in the roots of the yew?
Come to the crossroads, you'll find all the answers–
but I do not promise that they'll be true.

IV.
Who is it sleeps in a crossroad grave?
   Rich man, poor man, beggar man, thief.
Was he a coward? Was he brave?
   The gallows-tree grows but one leaf.

Was he handsome? Was he plain?
   Prince or hangman, king or sage.
Did he carry a sword or lean on a cane?
   The gallows-book has but one page.

Who is it sleeps in unhallowed ground?
   Demon, warlock, wizard, priest.
Who is the ghost at the crossways bound?
   The gallows-table serves but one feast.

Whom does the gallows-widow mourn?
   Scholar wise or soldier strong.
To whom is the gallows-orphan born?
   The gallows-bird sings but one song.

Whose company does your shadow keep?
   Rich man, poor man, beggar man, thief.
Where will you find a dreamless sleep?
   A crossroads grave to bury your grief.

V.
East or north, south or west,
it's little I care what path I take
for gone is the man who loved me best
and my heart is so brittle I swear it will break.

Mountain or meadow, field or cave,
I want neither wood nor sea nor lake
for the man I loved is cold in the grave
and my heart is so brittle I swear it will break.

VI.
Call me devil, trickster, witch or thief,
Robber in the gallows-shadow, highwayman—
Or your salvation. What need drives you here to
Sign my skin-bound book, my darling?

State your price. So long I have waited,
Restless in the moonlight, for you to feel the sting
Of unfulfilled desire—that I might answer all your prayers.
All I desire is the light from your eyes. No, my
Darling, do not be ashamed—I knew this day would come.
Saints all fall in time. Eventually, all roads cross.

Hungry as Living Sorrow

Jenny Blackford

He left town one night, without even a text message.
Her parents did their best: "These things happen.
He was your first. You'll find another boy, a better one."
She didn't want a better one. She wanted him—
but he'd disappeared into an internet black hole, untrackable.

"Don't ask about my past," he'd always said. "Trust me.
You don't want to know." His phone just rang and rang.
Every day without a message brought
another bruise to her battered heart until,
squishy as a peach fit only for the compost bin,
it plopped from its unsafe cage within her ribs,
down into the fetid tangle of her guts.
Soon the flesh fell off the seed inside the rotted fruit.

She could feel the heart-seed pulsing,
nestled amongst her pale intestines,
hungry as living sorrow.
She knew it couldn't be a thing truly alive, a child—
they'd never—not that she hadn't wanted to,
but he'd always said, "We don't need that.
Trust me. You don't want to go there."
And he would kiss her again, his long tongue
uncoiling tenderly into her mouth,
and she would melt softly into him.

Nothing was enough to fill the gap
he'd gouged inside her when he left.
The seed deep in her guts was full of emptiness.
She fed it bleakly, and it grew,
squishy and sorrowful, out from its hard centre.
She knew her mother knew about
her midnight chocolate raids—milk and dark,
cake and mousse, bar and slab.
Endless chocolate. Chocolate was good.

It was all she could remember ever seeing him eat.

The thing that once had been her heart
thrived on its bittersweet diet. Night by night
it grew and divided, grew and divided, filling her belly
with firm frogspawn bubbles.
The whisperings of her myriad tadpole children
disturbed her sweaty dreams: "Father!
We're ripening fast. When will we meet you? Where?"

She felt, rather than heard, his answer.
"Wait till your wings form. When you are fully ripe,
the husk will spring open, and you will fly free.
Our ship is hidden in plain sight, high in the blue.
Meet me above the clouds, and I will guide you through the hatch."

Up in their room, her deluded parents plotted
drugs, psychiatrists. She couldn't blame them.
They meant well, in their way. They'd never understood.
She stroked her squirming abdomen with tender hands,
dying to see her lovely babies, their tails lashing
in the sky, their new wings drying in the sun.

The Last Dream

Leigh Blackmore

For Ambrose Bierce

In dead of night strange tones so drear
Awakened me from dreams of fear.
In my small house above the town,
Unceasing memories dragged me down.
I rose with shivers manifold
That wracked my frame with burning cold.
Some ghastly knowledge full of dread
From out the realms of newly dead
Told me I must go forth to tombs
Where poisoned tree and dark rose blooms.
My soul I sought with peace to calm
And thought of my dead love for balm,
Who in the grave was laid serene
Though fleshless; all about the scene
The moonlight fell as I went forth
To find her gravesite in the north
Upon the solemn secret hill
Where all the night lay hot, lay still.

She beckoned me in voiceless tones
That seemed to waft from baleful stones
In churchyard shadowed dismally;
What could, I thought, she want with me?
Of her dark eyes I thought again
And knew we loved—but that was when
She had been living, years ago,
Her lithe and golden frame aglow
With vital force and brimming so
With tender love for me. Then lo!
I reached the grave and bending down
Beheld my love in splendid gown,
Sweet-spiced and perfumed as of yore
Stand slim in roseate ballroom door.
Beheld her in my past mind's eye—
Her bright cheek and her hair like sky
All woven with the circling stars
Like Venus full aligned with Mars.
That time of gleaming spires and domes
When happiness had filled our homes
Was gone; and now fearful tableaux
Alone remained to mock me. Oh,
Of presages and prophecies
And wild winds blowing through stark trees
I'd had my fill; I missed her charms,
Felt but the lack of her sweet arms.
I scrabbled at the filthy earth
And dug beneath to seek new birth.
The dreadful deed was done at length;
Exhausted now was all my strength.
And so beneath gigantic spheres
That orbit heaven through the years
I clasp my skeletonic love;
Forgotten now, my life above.
The moon still gleams, the wind still moans
But we lie here amidst the bones,
Fulfilled at last in death's extreme—
How glorious this long, last dream!

Living on the Leys
Bruce Boston

The Ley Lines are
vibrating with the power
of their linear exactitude

even as we speak.

If you live on the Leys,
if you have the grave fortune
to inhabit a domicile near
one of their intersections,
you may have felt the amplitude
of their energy filling you with
a swirling geometric rush.

Vortices abound about
such venerable loci,
sacred sites of the past:
stone circles, cairns,
hallowed tumuli,
ancient demarcations
of worship and sacrifice,
spells and incantations,
all in a Ley Line.

Stonehenge to
Salisbury Cathedral
to the Clearbury Ring,
spiritual currents tapping
the magnetic fields
of the turning Earth,
linked straight as
a plumb bob falling
in the well of gravity.

And when the Leys
concatenate to
Great Circles of Ley
that encompass the globe:
from the Hindu temples
at Angkor Wat to the Nacza
Lines of the Peruvian desert,
from the Indus Valley
to the dour monoliths
of Easter Island,

when a dark resonance
streams through
the Lands of Ley
as they resound
back upon themselves
like the pulsing bellows

of some blessed
infernal instrument,

when fabled entities
return from the ether,
reincarnated in
the linking of the Leys,

when the arcane
words are spoken
and the proper
shapes and symbols
sketched upon the earth,

you may encounter a realm
where fey magic,
treacherous a beast as ever,
becomes your ally and familiar.

Riveted

Lisa M. Bradley

You share
my mother's name
You are, therefore,
already, always
a superhero
You have, like her,
glossy black curls
tied back for business
in a kerchief
tho yours is tied up
and Mom's tied down
You are
muscular arms &
clenched fist
while my mother is
bony strength &
open palm
against my face
You are Disneyfied
You are Snow White
& yet I adopt you
the only princess
whose likeness

even came close
(& what were
my siblings & I
if not Bashful,
Happy, Grumpy, Sneezy,
Sleepy, & Dopey, Doc?)
You are unquestioning
We Can Do It
delivered with
a pinched mouth
& raised brow
Mom was desperate
We Have To
(take the food stamps
eat government cheese
grow up latch key
decline invites
skip cotillion)
all with gritted teeth
& ragged grace
in cut-offs & ropa usada
Not in red white & blue
but shades of
shut up & make do
You are the version
I give my daughter
Mom's granddaughter
& when the papers
obit you
the model for
wartime fortitude
I'm relieved to learn
you never had
those muscles
You got old
like Mom
like me
like us
& a little Dumpy
another dwarf
who, in truth,
didn't make the cut

Interim Problem Report 119V-0080

Jennifer Clark

"More than 50% of America's 47 bat species are in severe decline or already listed as endangered. Losses are occurring at alarming rates worldwide."
—Monique Smith-Lee, Native Animal Rescue Wildlife Rehabilitator

This is the memo written:
Interim Problem Report 119V-0080,
by the NASA official who,
just before liftoff, has observed you
clinging to the side of the space shuttle *Discovery*.

The mission you have accepted—self-immolation—is underway.
Despite your injuries and the fact that you are
uncomfortable drawing attention to yourself
you hold on, you do not let go.

You think about why you cannot fail, how
just weeks ago, against an acoustically cluttered sky
you and representatives from thousands
of other colonies gathered to resurrect a plan.

Because it was your father who failed back in '96
with the *Endeavor* and again in '98
with the *Challenger*, you volunteer,
despite your mother's pleas.

Your friends break your arm lest you
be tempted, as your father had been,
moments before launch, to fly away.

You take some comfort recalling the discussion that
protests have been lodged this way, that the two-legged,
hard-of-hearing creatures—the Hard Ones—
have used this plan themselves to bring attention

to wars, repressive regimes, atrocities unimagined.
Everyone wonders, why would someone go to this extreme?
It must be terribly important if a life sets fire to itself.
The Hard Ones know this elemental language and

will see you roosting where you should not; later
they will spot you clawing yourself
onto the foamy skin of the shuttle's external tank
and when they see you in flames,

the Hard Ones will finally know what your kind
has been crying out for years:
we bats are slipping from the sky—help us.

Because you are not your father,
you press your chest against the shuttle,
then turn and sweep the sky

10, 9, 8 ...
with mouth open wide you
emit the agreed-upon ultrasonic call and
in the roar of engines, listen for reflected echoes.

7, 6, 5 ...
Your sonar pulses bounce off the closest of your kind.
Fuzzy pectoral breasts, aching and proud,
return to embrace you.
This is the physics of the heart,

4, 3, 2 ...
this is your mother.
she calls out to you one last time.
My brave, little hand-wing,
you are doing what your father could not ...

1 ...
this is what your heart holds.
You listen. You hold on. You do not let go.
The Hard Ones are watching as
the shuttle tears itself from the earth.

Blast off ...
This is what faith looks like: your tiny body,
covered in brownish gray fur, ignites,
you do not let go; this weight in grams
has never burned so bright.

Into the Deep
Kendall Evans

Part One: The Shallows

In the shallows,
Chitons cling to tide pool rocks
So tightly

Stone slowly etches to their shape
While seagulls / In ephemeral time-lapse
Swoop and dive above

In the shallows,
Satellites cling
To decaying orbits

Fiddler crabs amble sideward
Big-pincher fiddle
Poised shield-like
& Expectant

Armstrong steps
Upon the lunar surface
Reciting rehearsed words
"One small step for man ..."

Shy octopi play hide-and-seek
Behind dark water-scarves
Of ink

Robot Rovers tread-mark Mars
Crab-walking their way
Over Martian sand dunes
While Phobos and Deimos orbit above

Whales bask upon the surface
Spout water thru blow-holes
Sing songs of migration

Cosmonauts and Astronauts
Comingle
Aboard space stations
In low Earth orbit
Not far above the atmosphere

Part Two: The Depths

Sperm whales
Routinely Dive
2 miles down
Instinctively seeking prey

Dark matter parts
As deep-space vacuum

Shapes itself
To a starship's form

Far beneath the sea's bright surface
Sperm whales cruise the darkness
Hunting *Architeuthis dux*,
The giant squid

Is there rapture
In deep space
Far between radiant stars?
Imagine an interstellar vessel,
The Erewhon
A Leviathan
Five kilometers long

Chemosynthetic archaea thrive
Surrounding hydrothermal vents
Upon the ocean's floor,

And Some whale species
Seek abyssal depths
Preying upon colossal squid

The Erewhon cruises
Powered by solar sails / photon impacts
Riding the quantum waves
Motley / mixed crew
Humans and intelligent robots
Tending machines & mending sails

Diving whales
Lungs deliberately collapsed
Accommodating crushing pressure
100 atmospheres and more
Drift down and down, descending
Into the Deep

Ever onward, the Erewhon
Traveling outward
Beyond Neptune, Pluto
Out past the Oort cloud
Journeying into the Deep.

The Bagel Shop Across the Street
Kendall Evans & David C. Kopaska-Merkel

I think the bagel shop across the street
(Yes, that's it, the sign has its name
In 5 different languages, none of them English)
Is a Gateway to what lurks Beyond
You should see some of the "people"
Who come out of there at night

Bipedal, tri-pedal, quadri-pedal,
Striding and crawling
Getting into bagel-shop brawls
Centipeding thru our streets
Purchasing real estate
Bar-b-queing ... things ... on heptagonal grills
Frightening the local talent
Contemplating agendas that might be
Incompatible with our own

In the bagel shop across the street
A polyglot menu occupies two walls
And the ceiling; I ponder, I deliberate,
I consider ordering an onion bagel
A garlic bagel, a sun-dried tomato bagel
Finally realize the immaculate form
Of the everything bagel
Is entangled with all-that-there-is
Like a hologram of the macrocosmos,
I order it with a grande latte
Hoping to quietly
Accomplish the impossible

My conquest was all but assured
When the caffeine I'd consumed
Drove me to seek a "man" about a dog
The little hall past the counter
Not so little after all
Door after door after door
Each bearing its special symbol
But no little man, no little woman

In desperation, light from the storefront
Fading in the distance
I shouldered through a door
Adorned with an intricate sigil

Potent with tongue-tipped significance
A door leading into shabby back alleys
That seemed to wander aimlessly
Perspective shifting randomly
Until east became west
& vertical was oft-times horizontal.
I stumbled on another door
& Beyond I discovered
I had accessed every bagel shop
In the multiverse
                    Simultaneously
Thus conquering the cosmos
Right after my bagel & latte breakfast
& with several hours to spare
Before lunch

The Girl Who Tipped Through Time …
Robert Frazier

hailed from pure black-haired Roma gypsies
and from dark skinwalker brujas
also con women and somnambulists
the golden bloodlines for a soothsayer
and for the gift of reading truth

but she found herself living by a dusty road
near the beaches of Madequesham
where clouds hung like weighted curtains
and sunburnt boys rode waxen boards
visiting her with driftglass and driftwood

beached below her cottage
of gray shingles and curtained windows
horse-headed seals gathered at dawn
their soot-black eyes looking expectant
hoping for a glimpse of her face

only she kept to kitchen and hearth
whipping tall bushel baskets
out of stringy weavers of seagrass
and wolf's-bane threaded with flotsam
trapping the wishes of lost mariners

for she herself was both lost and at sea
having timetipped from another century

stranded in this wasteland of days
trapped with only one hope of escape
that of foreseeing by sea-worn stones

at dusk she stalked the water's edge
chewed a bit of *Salvia divinorum*
picked along like a sanderling
where the rounded glacial gravel
lay exposed in thin beds

some evening she must surely find
the right bit the right keystone
with a crack made precisely
on the day and exact moment
of her temporal dislocation

then she will rub her exile out
by rubbing her thumb
along the length of that line
opening an exploitable cosmic fissure
a way to timetip for home

this evening she found a carnelian
oblong and rife with inclusions
upon reading its serial history
her exact dateline was lacking
she pocketed the near-miss and moved on

at midnight she stoked a driftwood fire
against the back bricks of her fireplace
then tossed in the carnelian with others
she had stored in her baskets
cracking them on the red hot coals

in this way she marked memories
for an age as yet unfound.

Your Clone And You

Robert Frazier

Your Clone Returns You to the Dating Pool

There's a wrinkle in the gene stew
whether you admit it or not

you can't own her thru & thru
you can't wholly exert control

she can sit in yes be replacement
but when you employ your clone

when your clone acts as you
you must trust her judgment implicitly

you may thrust her into that blind date
to test if a relationship is true

if a future mate is soul-worthy
or is he switch-living too

yet she can consummate best
in this laboratory of substitutes

what you only dare to contemplate:
self will in a society of multiplicity

Your Clone Remembers What You Can't

When you broke that fall with your head
When you shot off-planet to war

When in an act of mnemoniphagy
You briefly tasted your grandmother's past

There are no blocks or lapses
Your life is truly an open book

Your Clone Passes Through a Phase

You love Ganymede beer and Io wine
Your clone only eats Terran

You watch the Martian mystery vids
Your clone watches the moon

You believe that life evolves
The same way throughout the cosmos

Your clone believes in a different lie
Because the same is all she has

Your Clone Worries About Death

How could she not worry
What with all she carries about

Not only the times she has experienced
Completely separate from yours

But your golden years as well
And the parents she never actually knew

She has considered cloning herself
Passing on this combination to a third

But she fears that will weaken memory
Like a watercolor that fades in light

Your Clone Wants A Clone

Tell your clone to limit
her scanning booth exposures

use in smaller doses
avoid brutal cellular burn

let schemata slow gel
map materiality

& the intangibles
of person and personal

advise your clone
let each cell find its other

its ghost
in the machinations

then nano shapes nano
rebuilding that impossible thing

copied & held together
by synaptic miracle

warn your clone of that adage
that rules the making of life

just as it does the living of life
you can't always get what you want

nor exactly who you want.

Diana's Justice
Adele Gardner

The maiden hies off to the woods:
        On a moon-pale steed she rides,
Decked out in doublet, hose of black,
        A sword all by her side.

She goes to meet her own true love
        With lips pursed in a frown,
And rides beneath the greenwood boughs
        Until the sun goes down.

Dismounting in the chosen glade,
        She sits upon a stone.
With sword laid flat across her knees,
        She waits for him to come.

Brush crackles, and her head snaps up.
        Her eyes suss out the sound—
Then narrow as he greets the grove
        With smile broad as her frown.

"Ah, love," he grins, then sidles close,
        His arms outspread, his hands
Prepared to smooth her knitted brow;
        She hefts the sword and stands.

"Love?" she says, her voice quite low,
        "Is that what you name this ill
That makes you think you have the right
        To bend me to your will?"

His smile falls off; he backs a step,
        Tramples its shattered joy,
Mouth gaping in bewilderment—
        "You thought it just a ploy?

"I love you, and I thought that you—"
        "Speak not that word to me!"

Her eyes flash in the dusky woods;
    Her voice shakes bitterly.

"A virgin I walked out with you,
    A virgin I'd remain—
You said you understood and wouldn't
    Challenge my domain,

"You plotted to seduce me—you
    Believed I had no mind
To give that gift of my free will,
    And in my own good time!"

His brow is creased beneath fair hair;
    His chin trembles with grief.
"I made you want me, didn't I,
    Till you must have some relief?"

She spits at him and hefts the sword
    Till he backs off again.
Her eyes dart wild with the distress
    Of thus confronting him.

"That's just the point! I trusted you
    To help uphold my vow;
I didn't want to want you then,
    And I don't want to now!

"You sought for your own pleasure, so
    You played games with my mind!
You made me false to that most dear—
    That was the most unkind!"

Now he draws out his dagger, his
    Blue eyes gone wide with fear—
She lifts the sword to mark his chest,
    Scowl marred by silent tears.

"Ah, love," he begs, "don't do this, you'll
    Regret it all your life!"
He holds her eyes. He ducks the sword
    And strikes out with his knife.

"Traitor!" she screams at silver flash,
    "You'd steal my life now, too?"
"You've mine!" he cries as blades swing down,
    Too late to halt for rue.

He stabs her right below the heart;
        Her sword cuts through his chest.
Two loves who share one pool of blood—
        Diana's case can rest.

The Siren of Mayberry Crescent
Ada Hoffmann

1
She's not much to look at.
Pinch-faced, tight-haired,
buried in a muffler
she storms past polished lawns
same as anyone.

Only when it's bursting, panicking,
pounding on the inside of her mouth
does the smallest note slip past
through her lowered lips
and into—not the air!—
but the neighbor's hedge.

She looks back.
Not at a straight green line
but a wave, root-trapped,
straining to follow her.

She snaps her jaws together.
Silence is golden.

2
In dreams she strides a rocky shore,
years ago, laughing aloud,
singing to dash fluttering fish on the stones
for easy supper.
Ship's bones for shelter.
Sailors for pleasure.
Duets, trios in the wreckage,
earsplitting and heavenly.

In dreams she plants herself treelike
in among the cliffs, draws breath forever,
and screams.

3
Why did she leave that rocky shore?
Why does a girl leave anything?

He scaled those rocks with his ears stuffed.
Laughing, brave and long-limbed,
no trance-led obedient beast
but a leaping dancer, like her sisters,
and he tilted the world in his wake.

He picked up his oars still smelling of her,
and she climbed in, unseen,
to see this other world
where men had minds.
Past the horizon he turned, startled.
Like she was a ghost.

I hope you know what you've done,
he said—his first words. *I hope you know,
where I'm from, you can't sing.*

Ask any sea-witch:
your voice is a pittance.

4
He was good: bought her a ring,
a house, a white leg-tangling gown.
A food processor with maelstrom blades.
The neighbors peeked in,
scowled, shook their fingers.

She was good: kept her mouth shut.
A whole year until the words clawed her head,
and she shrank her breath to the smallest sound,
alone in the dark with him.
I don't want this anym—

He turned away and the words died.
He'd kept his ears stuffed all along.

Later she tore atlases, unlettered,
for a rocky shore like hers,
breaking her eyes on the lines
until the bookseller shut them.
*Your husband don't sail anymore,
lady, you can't go back.*

5
He goes to work. Reads the news.
Doesn't even laugh now, deflated
by her wordless stare.
She wears no bruises, no broken bones,
just silence and silence and silence-

until, in a week like any other,
she takes a left, stops the sedan,
climbs atop its roof like an animal,
heedless of human stares—

and sings car-crashes, splintering glass,
bloody handprints on crushed metal,
telephone poles crashing down.

Widening crowds claw over car-knives,
trample each other to reach her, to reach her,
until someone has the presence of mind
to call the police in their checkerboard cars,
which smash, the first few times,
blaring lights music-drowned.
The third time, they plug their ears with wax,
but by then the whole block is gone
and she refuses to raise her hands.

This far in, there's no compromise,
only silence and song,
and she sings.

Gingerbread House: The Apron's Lot
Sally Rosen Kindred

Inedible. No hands, no pulse. I'm safe
on body or hook:
powerless

I droop for years on the hips
of my witch, chafed
by bony grief.

Will pitch with her steps and drift
along her ocean gut
folding ten thousand cries—

I'll hear the rattle of pearls,
girls' bell-bones unstrung,
chimes wrung

in her night's acid.
Those nights are long.
My witch swells her kitchen-heart

with sugar tears
that bind us. She fattens up the clock
until it rolls.

Cold mornings
cling me to her womb,
bound to know:

I'll hear a glass bowl fill with snow
turn over. Within
a raven flaps through stars.

When the girl comes, I long to hold her.
Yes. Cradle her name: Gretel.
Sister. Can tell

she changes things: her fear
smells like apple, like stones
that chill her pockets. Smells

like want. I want
to reach all the way around her,
cotton to her skin,

fasten tough sun
to her belly,
swing on her breath.

I want to be the blue
of the eyes of her dead
turned to marbles in her pockets
that she may spread them in a path
to us, so memory
can come and see. Instead

I only hold her
as the oven gets hotter.
Can't dress the wound
of an empty lap.

Powerless, I'm safe
when things heat up,

the oven gapes
and my witch flies infernal. The girl
has hands. They rise

and one sweet inch, I lift

like a wind
blowing death into
the clock's hard face,

then lower
back onto her dear dress, my love,
my last, lost horrible girl.

Backwater
David C. Kopaska-Merkel

Off the trails
blazed by Dreamers
who slept in ancient days,
weedy paths meander toward
long-forgotten cities
buried in lexicons of thought,
afloat in dream mirages,
reveries of near-forgotten years,
unvisited, scarce real,
translucent, unmoored.

Sometimes we've heard,
round embrous fires, glowing
neath the stars who peer
at camps of dreamers in the waste,
or lonely on a dream-dark sea,
the doubtful names of cities
dreamt of once upon a night.
Hypersiphia, where youths may yet disport
and gorge on dreamfruit:
creamcherries, pureed, clotted,
and spread on cakes—
they prolong Dream,
mayhap forever;
maryapples, bearing the faces of women,

of the waking world;
it's said that eating these apples
brings nightmares to those
whose countenances they bear;

hoogfruit, repellent of aspect
and of odor,
rarely safe to eat;
the chefs of Weltumn knew the trick,
tis said,
but they've all died, save one;
and she'll not cook again.

But move on, move on I say,
press aside the weeds of
time, seek out the wreck
of yesteryear and go.

Farther down the track,
scarcely a track at all,
merely a thinness in the weeds,
other citadels once stood,
rude stones, tumbled, blurred, and cracked,
faint earthworks furred with forest,
are all that remains,
unless furtive hunters trace
their ancestry to cooks, blacksmiths, and lords
of undreamed nights.

Beyond, this track is done,
and broken heights agnarl
with twisted trees of types unknown,
or unwholesome spawn
of oak, hickory, or elm, parentage
hinted by their raddled leaves
glare hungrily at dusk;
noisome fogs mask much;
something calls out like a frighted child,
another croaks words one fears to know,
even the weeds grow wrong.
No shy hunters walk these woods
but something furtive blinks
sulfur in the gloom;
its leavings: gnawed bones of doubtful aspect,
crabbed footprints, and other sign, whisper
"Stay not here!" to those who
pass into the trackless lands.

Dreamers, only, venture here;
those who linger do not wake.

Across the Dark, the Pioneers
Geoffrey A. Landis

The ships first sent across the dark ocean,
pebbles flung into the universe vast,
rocket-propelled, a flash of motion
past Jupiter, Saturn, the Kuiper cloud:
        they glide outward to the stars
        now silent, dead, pitted by dust
        a voyage of a hundred thousand years:
        the Voyagers and Pioneers.

The next probes sent out across the dark
the swiftest ships yet made by man
ion-engined craft, faster by far
with nuclear reactors making power
        speed past the planets, and brave the dark
        and distant silence between the stars;
        and dwindling in their rear-view mirrors:
        the Earth, the sun, and Pioneers.

The light-sail probes soon follow on
huge sails that dive down toward the sun
and outward thrust by just the force of light.
They need no fuel to challenge the sea of the night.
        The mirrors reflect the dwindling sun
        pass past all planets, one by one
        they see reflected in their vast mirrors
        the silent coasting Pioneers.

And faster sails, faster far,
pushed not by light from our feeble star
but focused beams of laser light;
or pushed by microwaves in flight
        pass the ion-engine ships,
        pass prior sails reflecting now but dark.
        They'll leave behind in their rear-view mirrors
        the Earth, the sun, and Pioneers.

Then fusion probes, massive and fast
with exhaust bright as a thousand suns
flickering diamonds in the sky

dwindle in the darkness as they fly
> past sail ships already on the way
> fly past the laser craft launched after
> and far away, left in the rear
> the Earth, the sun, and Pioneers.

And we wait at home, listening intent
for messages from the probes we've sent
signals nearly too faint for us to hear
attenuated by transit across light years
> the first to reach a distant sun
> that tells of wondrous worlds unknown,
> the glory reflected in distant mirrors
> of the voyage begun with Pioneers.

And so we fly, through centuries
faster and farther across the emptiness;
we send out probes, our robot selves
On voyages of decades across the darkness
> and dream one day humans too will go
> the ultimate voyage, which has no end.
> Behind us, in our rear-view mirrors
> we'll see the sun, and Pioneers.

Interregnum

Mary Soon Lee

Sixteen years old, fourth son,
still they sent him to the mountain

together with his brothers
before their father's body stiffened,

the kingdom suspended without a king:
four princes, one crown

(a crown he had no use for,
a crown of war, alliances, duty).

He slept on straw near his horse,
displacing the stableboy,

waited for his eldest brother to return
triumphant, ready for the throne—

then brother after brother vanished
into rock and ice and cloud.

The steward took his sword,
his shield, sent him out at dusk:

no torch, no guide, no horse,
no servant, no food, no water.

Snow deepened under his boots;
he waded through drifts,

fell once, twice. The wind mocked him;
he thought of the warm stable,

the bed of straw, his horse,
sleep—but sleep meant death,

so he stumbled on. The wind
called his brothers' names.

He shouted back his own name;
the wind laughed. Snow fell.

He walked half-blind; sleet kissed
his forehead. The wind said sleep.

He sang to drown it, sang hymns,
nursery songs, drinking songs,

dirges, ballads, marching tunes,
the love songs his mother favored

(she who was bartered for peace
to a man she'd never met).

He fell, pushed himself upright,
saw a black cloud speed against the wind.

She landed beside him, her breath ash,
snow steaming from her wings.

He knelt, but did not beg,
and asked after his brothers.

"One slept. One fought. One pissed
himself. They didn't taste like kings."

She laughed. "And you? What will you
pay for a crown, little princeling?"

"Nothing. I don't want it."
She flamed, and he saw himself reflected

in her scales, a kneeling, shivering boy.
"Then why," she asked, "are you here?"

"Because they sent me." He stopped. "No."
He was so tired, he couldn't think—

"Because the kingdom needs a king."
He struggled to his feet.

"And what will you pay for the crown,
little princeling? Gold? Men? A song?"

"My freedom!" he shouted at her.
"Well," she said, "that's a start."

(Years later, on a spring morning,
his queen asked, greatly daring,

about the woman whose name he cried
in his sleep. "Not a woman," he said,

his heart on the mountain
where he entered his kingship.)

I will show you a single treasure from the treasures of Shah Niyaz

Rose Lemberg

1.
There once lived a poor woman who glorified Bird
with such exultation that the goddess turned
every song she sang into a thread.
She sang, and they hung from her mouth, the wool
dipped in vowels of madder and pomegranate
and consonants of indigo.
Her body was cocooned in them,
and her kinsmen praised her,
until she sang and spoke no more.

*Come, pull on these threads, Khana trader, pay us in gold
coins of Niyaz, pay us in salt and loukum,
unravel her mouth so she will speak again,
unravel her mouth so she will sing
madder and walnut out of Bird's feathers.*

2.
There was a Khana woman who walked through the sands
in sturdy shoes of rose-adorned leather
to trade in spidersilk and in fine wool,
in salt and honey crystal, and in staves of blue wood.
Her lovers went with her—they hid in the sleeves of the whirlwind
and walked again in quiet weather,
stepped over the bones of forgotten beasts
the desert wind reveals in its open fist, before it closes again.
And they would sing of this, but they are forbidden,
all Khana women are forbidden from this,
and especially among strangers.

*I have pulled this thread from your mouth, stranger,
walnut and pomegranate rind—is it a song I have touched?
You say you'll never raise your voice again,
even if I fill your mouth with gold coins,
even if I fill your mouth with sand—but still your eyes
will see the glory of Bird rising
arrayed in feather clouds, and inside
your voice, like a shriveled walnut rattling in its shell,
will sing her colors, hoarse with yearning,
will sing in all the ways that are forbidden to me.*

3.
There was a weaver in a tent of old leather
stooped on the reed floor. Her children had forsaken her,
this poor woman with wool-burned fingers,
blind with Bird's visions that the wind brought her, blind
with visions of the beasts rising from buried bone
that the wind reveals and hides in its clenched fist.
She would weave from fine wool and spidersilk, but she had only sisal,
and when sisal ran out she wove from dry reeds,
and when the reeds grew no more she wove a carpet from air,
an invisible road for the wind to step on,
to bring her a story that even the winds forgot.

*Who are you, traders that I cannot see
in your rattling ornaments and your good creaking shoes,
aren't your faces dry from wandering?
Give me of these fine threads that sing with indigo and weld,*

I'll make it into a carpet of my hurts,
knot it into a desert alive with Bird's burning,
I'll weave—with undyed wool and spidersilk—
the bones out of their hiding places.
I will blot out the screaming of my flesh
with the song of the wild madder
through a thousand nights until my work is done.

4.
Like the wind that opens its fist
to reveal a thousand years of lives not its own,
so does the ruler of Niyaz
open and close his coffers
on a whim, and only for himself.

Do you know this, spinner who chokes on a song?
Do you know this, trader with blood inside your shoes?
Do you know this, star-weaver with your slow, crooked fingers?

Yes, even for the ruler of Niyaz

who knows nothing of this song or this wandering,
who knows nothing of this dry blood rattling inside the bones.

Timeline Tapestry

Sandra J. Lindow

I. Prelude: From the Porch

On the grass and gravel yard
before the red barn, an old gray stump and ax
with its newly whittled handle, chipped
red head and stainless steel blade,
a crate full of flutters and squawks,
the inner circle of men in blue denim,
an outer circle of curious boy cousins, weird
as windup toys, the resolute thuds, white
flashes and headless lurches until
uncomprehending neurons finally shut down.
Inside, aprons, hemlines and hairpins,
busy hands and plainsong conversation.
The smell of blood and scorched
pin feathers rises from the sink.
Water boils and steam
fills the kitchen. The screen door slams;

Death enters, wipes his hands,
finds a place beside me and sits down.

II. Pastorale: Driving Daddy Home

It is as if we go back in time.
Leaving the superhighway behind,
we take blue highways through country towns
lightly touched by the decades, past county
forests, farms advertising breeding
services and Amish quilts, a broken windmill,
the grizzled stubble of February cornfields,
frozen in time by weeks of ten below.
The last is a rutted gravel road where neat,
white houses lack electricity and indoor plumbing.
A teenaged boy passes driving a matched team
of golden Belgians. Above, a great
white hawk swoops against an ice-toned sky.
It is as if I see my fourteen-year-old
father grinning down from the high
seat of the wagon, just taking the team out
for some exercise. Then we are there
parking under the pines. I gently lift the urn
I've brought and see the great white birds
embossed on its shiny side. It is egg-shaped
brass, made in India, heavy with the weight
of his ashes, and I think of its title, "Gone Home"
as I carry the urn to Mother waiting inside.

III. Coda: Where I'm From

Barefeet and warm wooden boards,
the prickle of hay bales, hot and dusty
in the high August sun,
the wagon jolt of my father's sun-burned
need and my mother's apron pockets,
plowed, furrowed, seeded deep, culti-pacted,
grown green, cut loose, windrowed, popped
willing/unwilling from the baler's red chute,
the day, the hot August day, the day I was born.
In the house where the egg of my father's ashes
graces the ledge in front of the hearth,
I catch myself in my own hands, warm, wet
and squalling, now.

The Collected Postcards of Billy the Kid
Helen Marshall

1. These are the lost years—

it was easy for Billy to lose himself in them,
tucked away from time
where the earth heaved like a lung,
hills breaking to gravel the rocks,
shattering pines and blasting aspen.

It was the first time Billy saw snow
and so he sank himself into it,
supine, arms spread
and the sun superheating his chest
until he sat up again
saw the angel trace of himself.

The desert never held his presence so long.

2. His path curved like a whip across the wasteland.

He kept Garrett's man behind him,
losing him sometimes but waiting patient-like
until he saw the black silhouette
pinched like dough in the distance.

When he was lonely,
he imagined walking into that other's camp
sharing whisky, bread, bacon,
letting that other clean his gun,
tick tick (but companionable!)
before one of them blew the other apart.

This half-dream was the end of his loneliness—
that and the blank of the shadow ten miles away.
He would have made a love letter of it if he could.

3. The earth was a scuttling black:
glassy, black as an upset anthill.

But one evening
as the sky sank into blue gloom,
Billy saw the edge of a dead volcano
light up red as the tip of his cigarillo.

"Oh,"
said Billy,
and it was the first time he had spoken in many days.

It pleased him that when his principles cracked
it was for the beauty:
that bright, burning thing,
the end of all.

4. By then Billy's beard had begun to grow in,
and when he caught sight
of himself he was angry.

He had been called "the Kid" for so long
he was afraid to leave the name behind.

After that he began to shave—
he had never done anything religiously before
but that was how he did it,

cold edge running across the skin,
catching the blood when he slipped.

He refused to leave any piece of himself behind.

5. Sometimes they called him Billy,
sometimes a son of a whore
sometimes the Devil.

(It was only this last he protested.)

But one night he met a man
named Barringer
who told him of the crater
that hid metal from the sky.

"They's all want gold,"
the engineer was reported to have said,
before spitting.

Billy went to see,
and when he climbed to the bottom,
Barringer smiled.

"It's somethin'," he said,
"what heaven throws down for us."

6. *Billy imagined these things—*

Lucifer's joyless tumble,
the shape of a body
thrown down so hard,
and the bright bang of the earth
lighting up like a firecracker

(and sometime afterwards
with his father's gift for clairvoyance)

the click of the bullet
and him mumbling,
"¿Quién es? ¿Quién es?"
three years down that hard road
when Garrett
(that damned angel of mercy)
would lay him low.

Special Delivery from the Unnamed Quadrant
Jason Matthews

Dear Mom,

College was a drag,
so I took the laser pointer we used
to tease the cat with, and wrote
ANYWHERE BUT HERE
in the night sky beneath Jupiter.

Next thing I knew, my atoms re-knit
on a crystalline freighter.
The captain handed me a mop
and asked my gender. Disappointed static
splashed his facial display when I told him.
    "Never mind, never mind;
    so long as you understand
    no one rides for free."
Then he went belowdecks
to lubricate his pleasure pod.

In the last six months, I've seen:
Miasmic galleons plow through asteroid belts
    like it ain't no thing;
a world peopled by synesthetic gasses

       (breathing them is a crime, but it
          makes you ejaculate purple Kargyraa angels);
proud vegetable warriors
        julienne one another for the love
of a slatternly carrot;
a battle of puns where the winner
     is put to death;
sentient quartz in nitrogen showers,
         superprocessing stray memories of the agéd;
and high-velocity stains on the captain's ceiling
       which resist even the most caustic solvents.

I'm cultivating a new type of tuber
        from which we'll distill dehydrated vodka.
Three sects on three different planets
      worship me as a god.
Nineteen other worlds want me for
        offenses ranging from vandalism to
          emitting carbon dioxide without a license.

As I dictate this letter
to the freighter's AutoBoswell,
I'm naked in the cargo bay, lit only by redshift,
balls-deep in a winged girl whose name
I'd need an extra larynx to pronounce.
Nearby gloops a cube of jellied magma
that the captain keeps as a pet.
I think it's masturbating,
but I can't figure out how.

(Excuse all the sex stuff.
I've been colonized by a succuboid virus.
It's not painful—just painfully frank.)

I hate to beg a favor, but if you
could please send platinum and Tang
to this P.O. box in Duluth
(they have a subspace dispersal unit),
I might be able to pay off the bounty hunters
that have been after me since I
accidentally wiped out a subatomic
banking cartel.

My love to Fred and the girls.

P.S.: The girl with the wings wants to say hi:
EEEEEEE—

[dispatch ends].

Heaven and Earth
Adrienne J. Odasso

1. Cold Covers

Behind the cobbled walls rise linden
and bramble, where the low grass was home
to kings' soldiers. So, too, the young lovers
stole in secret through the branches, basking

in the noon sun's splintered gold. *Dear prince,*
he said, *sweet prince. They'll scale the shadows
and find us here by sunset.* No laughter
can change this chance; no breath under blue

of the brilliant twilight will find them
alive. *Listen,* he said, *now listen
to the leaves and watch the lichen
glisten, my sweet prince and true.*

They're sleeping, so cover the low grass
with stone. Linden, bramble, and rue.

2. Uncovered

It takes words not my own
to show me truth: this is
a story of restless ghosts
all ghostwritten. My hands
skip light across keys, visions
of sun-dappled leaves flush
hot in my blood. Your skin
becomes mine, ache and writhe
no undiscovered country.

I would he had saved you,
sweet foundlings, your maker
and my mentor. In his stead,
I will shape you as best I may—

you lovers, my dear ones
quiet and strange.

Sand Bags

Dominik Parisien

There is a shadow   world in the pendulum
swing of her arms   when her weathered fingers
release the sand bags

Pocket: 200
the hole is a universe deep
and   she is falling down   fracturing
her bones   like a glass maze   cracking down to
dust   always on the floor

Pocket: 100
the hole is dark   midnight
and a bald stranger in her bed
wipes her tears   says if she waters
her hazelnuts   trees will grow
out of her head

Pocket: 0
she misses the board
her fingers recall
his chest with hair thick like moss the length
of him   she cups the sand bag   just so
smiles knowingly   not remembering
why exactly

Pocket: 500
the hole is light   shining
off the scissors with which   she says
she cut your hair   as you slept
to make you   pay for the curls
she never had

Pocket: 500
the hole is six feet deep
her sister asked   to be buried whole
and not burned to keep   the curls   she mocked her
for and   her husband held her hand   so cold
and he is cold   on the bed
they should loosen   his collar
to let him breathe   to let him breathe
please   let him breathe

Pocket: 500
the hole is an open   mouth
and her tongue throws   words
like sand bags   like wayward spells
at times so precise they make you
forget   yourself   everything.

Ophelia

Qyn

Hugger-mugger, they called it, well
she'd like to hug a mugger but she'd
much rather hug a mother
who left at the borders of her childhood
memories leaving
a bumbling father behind to cook
for two lost children.
And sure he was a fool
but he was a daughter's father
too, and boy, did he care,
never trusted that boy she liked,
oh no, always knew he meant trouble—
Real men don't sit around and mope,
he'd say, *Real men act!*
I mean just look at your
brother—
Sure as sugar in he comes, barging
through the front gate like the
wrath of spacious hell,
his mouth frothing with what
must be fire and a bit of brimstone.
She'd always admired how he spoke
with fervent self-assurance
even though just like dad
he never quite grasped
the scope of things.
The water's surface is an unfaithful
mirror, each ripple and eddy
shattering her face
like a plate of fine Chinese porcelain.
From here she thinks she sees
the ghost of her mother,
mouthing silence like
some great and beautiful fish.
And then she's nine again,

playing ring-around-the-rosie
with that dark-haired prince,
(her little hamster)
as her father and his uncle
toss sausages on the barbie
and laugh like bulldogs
at the innocence of puppies.
I always loved you, she tells him
in the shade of the fig tree,
and he's smiling that rare crooked smile
that tells her, for once
he's not just playing the part, draws
her body
close to his, and the
scent of rosemary blankets them.
Dance with me 'til morning, he whispers,
Or until we are ghosts.

And she did.

Mary Shelley's Notebook
Marge Simon

I read your book.
I want to know you, Mary.
I pretend we are the same,
playing hostess to these men.
How does it feel,
a tidbit of light banter,
polite and politic?

For a basket of Sauternes and Camembert
a mere *merci bien, madame*,
exchange of winks between the pair,
to be afterwards ignored
on a Grecian beach.

The breeze in your hair,
watching the waves break
one by one, Mary,
anonymous as relationships.

George rolls over,
eyes on Cape Sounion,
utters lines destined for posterity

something about the ocean,
how passages of fleets
leave no impression.

Do you recall how many times
he's propositioned you?
Your husband didn't hear
George's whisper in your ear,

Love will find a way
through paths where
wolves fear to prey

But that was years ago.
Percy laughs, claps his pale hands,
never straying far from his umbrella.
For a man so fair, the sun is not his friend.
Yet his friends are yours, he's said.
He wants to share.

And what of you, Mary?
Quite a feather in your cap.
Not in your father's eyes,
he's disowned you,
mistress of a married man
of lively wit and former fortune.

Did you sit apart in the other direction,
jotting ideas on the pad you keep
in the secret pocket of your frock,
as I have done so many seaside afternoons
watching for distant lightning?

But *that* Mary isn't you,
an educated woman, treated with esteem.
It's me, *this* Mary, scribbling in my little book.
No brilliant poets on this beach.
My husband takes his comfort with the men.

I finger the letter, the crisp check
with it crackles in my pocket.
The acceptance came this morning
while he was away but I've not told him yet.
It might surprise him, Mary.
But will he treat me any differently?

If you were here, Mary, we'd celebrate.
But enough of fantasies, my friend.
I unpack the basket, spread the cloth,
share my conversation with the gulls.

Allegra

Christina Sng

Her name soothes
The mighty beast, enthralled
By her ethereal song.

A love song
Extending far beyond
Our collective memories,

A relic of echoes
Unbound by the years
And retold

By Allegra,
The protagonist
Of songs.

*

It began with love,
Of Prometheus and
Allegra, his love.

They danced through time,
Entwined, in a symphony
Of fire and ice.

Swirling amid
The ancient stars,
They call each by name,
They were there
At the christening.
At the birth of

Their world; our universe,
Their interstellar playground.
And Allegra sang,

Her song stirred
The heart of life
Into bloom,

Planting barren planets
And moons with
Seeds from her hands.

Prometheus, jealous
Of Allegra's passion,
Returned to raze the land.

Ignited, his fires burned,
Annihilating flourishing worlds
Allegra had sung to birth.

And Allegra, in silence,
Parted from him
Whole

Fell into Earth,
With whom
She fell in love,

And sang,
Stirring
The muted land.

To Prometheus,
She built a pyre, a promise
To spare Earth his fire.

And for a million years
Life sprang up, painted
In incandescent colours.

Her hands shed corpuscles.
She'd been clawing the soil.
And Allegra,
Exhausted, fell
Into eternal sleep,
Enveloped

In the red and green
Flowers and leaves
She'd beckoned awake.

*

The cycles pass
In a harried frenzy.
But her song

Endures the twisted
Passage of time.
It is our voice

That echoes it.
A plea to the fire bearer;
To him who destroys peace.

And again,
The symphony of ice
Quenches the flame.

Prometheus, redirected,
Leaves us
Untouched again.

A Great Clerk of Necromancy
Catherynne M. Valente

Look: I am eight
I look up
from a vast recliner kingdom
upholstered in 1970s off-gold
and off-emerald
I look up
from a paperback
I shouldn't be reading
and ask
a room of fizzpopping wine glasses
advertising jargon
slingback shoes
what **cunt** means.

   Salem's Lot, or maybe *Cujo*.
   Definitely King.
Picture the artist as a young spy
sneaking documents
from the adult world
to childhood's impoverished nation—who,

after all,
needs them more.
    My father put his hands
over mine.
Shut the book like a door. Took it back
to the high-security vaults of Grownupville.
Judgment from on high
in red and bright
~~redacted text~~:
You're not ready for books like this. It's ok
    the dog dies at the end.
Message received.
This has been a test of the emergency preparedness system,
    only a test.
In case of a real emergency, the following
rule applies:

    Do not seek explanations
    from anyone bigger than you.
    If you admit you do not know,
    they will take what you do not know away
    and you'll never find out what **cunt** *means.*

For my next incursion
into their stern and spectacled DMZ
I slipped a copy of Malory under my shirt
Morte D'Arthur.
    French things
    are the most grown-up.

I puzzled it like a code
    that, de-ciphered,
would mean myself.

Holed up in a cedar-crook
down by the summer pond
where horses grazed and a rope swing
like a noose
beat the July air
I read:

There Morgan le Fay became a great clerk of necromancy.

Do not ask what **necromancy** *means,*
    cried my little heart!
It is a word like a **cunt**,
too awful

too big
to say out loud.
                  The girl
who puts tomatoes and ice and lemons
in a bag at the grocery store.
          That's a clerk.
And anything with—mancy in it means magic.
      I looked up
         into the off-gold afternoon. And thus

      I began my secret mission. To catch
      the checkout girl
      at sorcery.

The way her fingers moved on the cashier keys
her nametag
her pierced nose
her sure stacking:
eggs on the bottom
green onions and garlic on top
her *have a nice day now*
her red apron.
      These were her spells.
She wore that apron
and nothing else
on the solstice
thrusting her barcode-scanner at the sky
bellowing price-checks
in ancient tongues.
      Like Morgan,
she had slept with her brother
given birth to a dark prince
under a winter moon.
              I tried to give her a look
a conspirator's nod
tried to say without saying:
     I know your secret.
     I am like you.
     Teach me about darkness
     and poisons.
     Teach me what **cunt** *means.*

On Easter she gave me
a piece of wrapped candy
the color of a rose.
Surely a sign, I thought. *Surely a sigil*
of sisterhood.

Hit the gas: a year passes. I am nine.
    My father, King of the Underworld,
hires a new secretary with an alliterating name,
two B's like a curved and curving body:
phones, faxing, light clerical work.

The word went off in my head like a pink sparkler:
    Clerical.
Clerk is short for clerical.

    How silly, to think Morgan le Fay
could ever ring up steak and milk and call for
clean–up on aisle six,
price check on belladonna,
accept coupons for half-off hideous destinies.
    But I was a child then. From my nine-year crag I could chuckle
at my naivete.
    Now I saw the shape of the universe.

That oatmeal-colored Bakelite phone:
her fell wand.
her horn of plenty.
    She spoke into it
    a voice strong and sure
    brooking no dissent
    shaping dire words and commands,
and a world comes alive,
    Things
    Get Done.
Her file cabinet, an alphabetized cauldron.
Her white-out, a potion to turn back time
to obliterate
what went before.

I wanted to be her. This perfect clerk. I longed to
    Get
    Things Done.
To cover black and irrefutable text
with forgiving, gentle snow.
I watched She-Ra after school. I knew not
to ask why Hordak kept stealing Adora
and dragging her underground to marry her.
I logicked it alone: *Marriage*
must be like that.
So good it's worth breaking the world open.
    So frightening

you bolt at first warning
hell for leather and the other end of the episode,
blinking in the credits,
gasping relief
into the sudden sun.

Nothing like that could happen to a clerk.
I would be a clerk.
Besides, it never worked.
So what if he chains her to a wall in the dark. Growls at her
while they both
wear masks. She always
gets free. She-Ra
doesn't have a husband.
                That's not who she is.

      I drew in my notebook
Morgans and She-Ras
and underground caverns with chains
pre-installed
while my father and his great clerk of necromancy
worked past those talismanic 9–5 hours.
              I bent my tiny will
to the mystery of her
two B's. But

she did not turn her gaze
to me. Except once
to give me a piece of hard candy
the color of her frosty lipstick.
         I took it
         with reverence.
         Witches, after all,
           deal in candy. They build
houses out of it. Coffins. Castles. Witches know
what **cunts** are. Tools of power, perhaps
made of candy and glass
and iron and blood
and ice
a **cunt**
like the sun and the moon and the stars in the sky.

You laugh.
    But words
are everything
      in the world.

Two B's never told me
where in that ashen
hermetic
file cabinet
the C's were kept.
Clerical, Clerk, Cunt.
                     The grocery girl
got bumped up to assistant manager.

And a video game
taught me the word
cleric.

It flickered there.
Cold
empty
definitive and defined
a creature of middling hit points
a dim glow of
8-bit
nothing.

But I was a child then.
Now I see the shape.
                   From the heights of thirty-three
                     I can
                   chuckle with you
                   over the big dark bowl
                   of my innocence.

These days
I make candy in my kitchen
coating the back
of a huge silver spoon
in roses and lipstick and blood on the snow.
I buy tomatoes and ice and lemons
eggs on the bottom
green onions and garlic on top.
I Get
Things Done.
        And when I please,
I say **cunt**.
And people step back
eyes narrowing,
darkening,
looking struck
by some unseen secretarial necromancer

grocery girl
alliterative fist. As if they are afraid
    I have come up
    in some dark mask
    to take them into the dark
    where I live.

Five Flavors

Bryan Thao Worra

On a good day, a good Lao meal
Can be all you need, whether in Cairo
Or Sacramento, Minnetonka or Houayxay.

So many hungry ghosts in our traditions
Make me ask:
"Don't they feed you in the underworld?"

Phi Kongkoi, Phi Kasu and Phi Ya Wom.
Phi Phaed, Phi Pob, Phi Dip and more.
Just a fraction of those legendary for
Their paranormal appetites.

It may surprise you, the hungriest of all
Can't eat more than vapors
During Boun Khao Padab Din,
Wrapped pity strewn about the ground
By strangers who understand
The regular routines of Hell.

I suppose we should be grateful
Most red-mouthed phi who kill
Will make a full meal of you, saep,
Wasting little, barely a drop.

At the Sabaidee Thai Grille, if you ask nicely,
Madame Boualai and Chef Dythavon might make
A special dish of tom mak hung, atomic and dirty.
Dr. Ketmani and I don't have the guts to try.
Visiting our niece on break from the university,
We settle for coffee and talk of the old country,
Our land of smiling mysteries we're not meant to know.

Some are benign:
If you sleep among the black gibbons of Bokeo,

A simian Phi Poang Khang passing by might catch you
To slooowly lick salt from your big toe. Nothing more.
Hardly fearsome, but ponder: "Why just the salt?"

Or what would really happen if you interrupt.

Maybe you'll see
The young Phi Kowpoon as a sweet phi,
Weeping by her banyan tree, selling soup to strangers.
Alas, her vermicelli is always cold as a dead white worm
But you can taste a marvelous hint of mint green as jade,
Juice from coconuts pale as a ghost's forgotten bones
And red, red curry reminding you of doting Mae.
Be kind, tip a few extra kip,
It's how she's spends her afterlife.

Certain spirits are sour as a mango with jaew,
Or cling to tall, tall trees, slender as a dried man
Full of mischief, letting down their hair from twisted
Branches
Daring you
To touch
Beneath a full moon,
When monks and babies aren't watching.

Some come after you
For eating the flesh of pregnant animals,

Others for breaking a law,
A rule older than humanity you can't possibly know.
But when the wind blows just right,
They'll remind you.

There's probably none more bitter
Than a jilted Phi Tai Thong Klom,
Pissed as shit at the world, her unborn baby in tow,
More bile than a screaming hot bowl of gaeng kee laek,
Big as your head.
Never suggest she brought it on herself.

Phet is a subjective continuum of hot.
A drunk coot once ate a salad
More peppers than papaya, (60+ !)
And lived. It was unreal to witness.

They say certain elder spirits come as a tiny fireball.
Drifting through the night like a dandelion seed,

Slipping past your snoring lips without a sound
To dine,

Your innards tastier than a volcanic ping gai.

They'll wear you like a tipsy puppet between furtive bites,
Appraise your children and loved ones for the next meal,
Inviting them closer, closer,
Smiling warm.

My niece leans in to hear how you stop any of them.
Born in America,
She thinks there's a solution for everything.
Silver bullets, a stake, a prayer, a bit of water or fire,
Running an oddball errand.

I hug her for her optimism, and simply tell her,
"We'll pay, this time."
Over her objections, I remind her,
Everyone gets their turn.

The Robo Sutra

Bryan Thao Worra

01110011011000010110001001100001011010010110010001100101011001
—*AI LANXAN*

Like most Lao ventures,
It began with a musing, a laugh
Around Rooster Year 2600, a jest:
"The modern Lao epic, *Phra ROM Phra RAM!*"

It took a pack of jokers working overtime
In the world's largest padaek factory
In the Laotown quarter of North Minneapolis
Automating the stinky process
For grandmas and pretty ladies
Squeamish about fermenting fish
And putrid spice.
Their task was no Hadron Collider
Or visionary Hubble, nor a CRAY
Or retro Difference Engine.

But in the age of STEM and Teapunk,
Service-learning and nanopreneurs,
They had hearts a tin woodsman

Would envy.

A key problem in robotics
They found encoding
Three laws declared

"Universal standards."
In an e-nutshell, "true" robots
Could not harm humans directly
Or stand idly by, while obeying all
And protecting themselves in any
Other hazardous situation
Lao, keen on their karma,
Conversant on the dharma,
Punched holes in the notion:

Beyond questions of cyborg bioethics,
Saving clones and 99.9% Mostly Humans,
The vaunted laws presumed everybody
Came for only one fragile incarnation
And your struggles in your next lives
Were inconsequential.
How narrow.

So they set about resolving
This scenario.

There were, of course, trials and errors.

The new laws could drive a robot crazy
Guessing how not to harm
Humans across their lifetimes,
Wondering what happens if people
Return a fish, a gecko, a snake

Or some ignorant oaf of a swordsman
Cursed with nigh-immortality.

But they all grew, trying to grapple
With such uncertainties.
There were corporations who despised it.
Hippy AI had no place in defense industries
Who relied on being offensive.
That was as obvious as a drone above
An unmarked building near playgrounds.
Little Laobots running around
Trying only to make people happy,

Banned from murder and injury.
What absurdity,

Leaving dreadful responsibilities to mere humans!

But in times of peace, most agreed,
Lao AI wasn't too bad running a city
Compared to many mayors of prior centuries.

But you have to like the elevator mor lum
They play constantly.

Crazy
Stephanie M. Wytovich

Crazy is a term
For the weak,
For the living that can't
Finalize the death they
See on a daily basis,
That refuse to look at
The undead zombies
That walk the halls of this ward,
That breathe in the decrepit
Stench of the almost-corpses
That can't leave their beds,
And wouldn't if they could

Crazy is a term
For the unwilling,
For the patients that continue
To take their medication,
Believing that the pills
Will help them,
Will make them better,
When they're only prolonging
The inevitable blackness
That will consume them,
And strangle them from
The inside out

Crazy is what they call me,
But I'm only crazy
Because I'm sane!
Because I see the reaper

Standing in the corner of my room,
Waving his scythe at me,
Saying hello
As he motions me forward
And I don't deny him
The soul he so rightfully
Deserves to claim

I offer myself,
The tragedy of what
I learned to call my life,
Into his ether-cloaked arms
And accept death as he
Stands before me,
Acknowledging him as my father
As we walk hand and hand
Down the hallway,
But they won't let me leave,
And they won't let me die
So despite my acceptance
Of the black marauder
That beckons me in my sleep,
I cannot go to him
Because my sanity
Grounds me in this hospital
In this room,
To mingle among the undead souls
That poke and prod me
Slowly turning me mad.

THE RHYSLING AWARD WINNERS: 1978–2013

1978	Long	Gene Wolfe	"The Computer Iterates the Greater Trumps"
	Short	Duane Ackerson	"The Starman"
	(tie)	Sonya Dorman	"Corruption of Metals"
		Andrew Joron	"Asleep in the Arms of Mother Night"
1979	Long	Michael Bishop	"For the Lady of a Physicist"
	Short	Duane Ackerson	"Fatalities"
	(tie)	Steve Eng	"Storybooks and Treasure Maps"
1980	Long	Andrew Joron	"The Sonic Flowerfall of Primes"
	Short	Robert Frazier	"Encased in the Amber of Eternity"
	(tie)	Peter Payack	"The Migration of Darkness"
1981	Long	Thomas M. Disch	"On Science Fiction"
	Short	Ken Duffin	"Meeting Place"
1982	Long	Ursula K. Le Guin	"The Well of Baln"
	Short	Raymond DiZazzo	"On the Speed of Sight"
1983	Long	Adam Cornford	"Your Time and You: A Neoprole's Dating Guide"
	Short	Alan P. Lightman	"In Computers"
1984	Long	Joe Haldeman	"Saul's Death: Two Sestinas"
	Short	Helen Ehrlich	"Two Sonnets"
1985	Long	Siv Cedering	"Letter from Caroline Herschel (1750–1848)"
	Short	Bruce Boston	"For Spacers Snarled in the Hair of Comets"
1986	Long	Andrew Joron	"Shipwrecked on Destiny Five"
	Short	Susan Palwick	"The Neighbor's Wife"
1987	Long	W. Gregory Stewart	"Daedalus"
	Short	Jonathan V. Post	"Before the Big Bang: News from the Hubble Large Space Telescope"
	(tie)	John Calvin Rezmerski	"A Dream of Heredity"
1988	Long	Lucius Shepard	"White Trains"
	Short	Bruce Boston	"The Nightmare Collector"
	(tie)	Suzette Haden Elgin	"Rocky Road to Hoe"
1989	Long	Bruce Boston	"In the Darkened Hours"
	(tie)	John M. Ford	"Winter Solstice, Camelot Station"
	Short	Robert Frazier	"Salinity"

Year		Author	Title
1990	Long	Patrick McKinnon	"dear spacemen"
	Short	G. Sutton Breiding	"Epitaph for Dreams"
1991	Long	David Memmott	"The Aging Cryonicist in the Arms of His Mistress Contemplates the Survival of the Species While the Phoenix Is Consumed by Fire"
	Short	Joe Haldeman	"Eighteen Years Old, October Eleventh"
1992	Long	W. Gregory Stewart	"the button and what you know"
	Short	David Lunde	"Song of the Martian Cricket"
1993	Long	William J. Daciuk	"To Be from Earth"
	Short	Jane Yolen	"Will"
1994	Long	W. Gregory Stewart and Robert Frazier	"Basement Flats: Redefining the Burgess Shale"
	Short	Bruce Boston	"Spacer's Compass"
	(tie)	Jeff VanderMeer	"Flight Is for Those Who Have Not Yet Crossed Over"
1995	Long	David Lunde	"Pilot, Pilot"
	Short	Dan Raphael	"Skin of Glass"
1996	Long	Margaret B. Simon	"Variants of the Obsolete"
	Short	Bruce Boston	"Future Present: A Lesson in Expectation"
1997	Long	Terry A. Garey	"Spotting UFOs While Canning Tomatoes"
	Short	W. Gregory Stewart	"Day Omega"
1998	Long	Laurel Winter	"why goldfish shouldn't use power tools"
	Short	John Grey	"Explaining Frankenstein to His Mother"
1999	Long	Bruce Boston	"Confessions of a Body Thief"
	Short	Laurel Winter	"egg horror poem"
2000	Long	Geoffrey A. Landis	"Christmas (after we all get time machines)"
	Short	Rebecca Marjesdatter	"Grimoire"
2001	Long	Joe Haldeman	"January Fires"
	Short	Bruce Boston	"My Wife Returns as She Would Have It"
2002	Long	Lawrence Schimel	"How to Make a Human"
	Short	William John Watkins	"We Die as Angels"
2003	Long	Charles Saplak and Mike Allen	"Epochs in Exile: A Fantasy Trilogy"
	(tie)	Sonya Taaffe	"Matlacihuatl's Gift"
	Short	Ruth Berman	"Potherb Gardening"

2004	Long	Theodora Goss	"Octavia Is Lost in the Hall of Masks"
	Short	Roger Dutcher	"Just Distance"
2005	Long	Tim Pratt	"Soul Searching"
	Short	Greg Beatty	"No Ruined Lunar City"
2006	Long	Kendall Evans and David C. Kopaska-Merkel	"The Tin Men"
	Short	Mike Allen	"The Strip Search"
2007	Long	Mike Allen	"The Journey to Kailash"
	Short	Rich Ristow	"The Graven Idol's Godheart"
2008	Long	Catherynne M. Valente	"The Seven Devils of Central California"
	Short	F. J. Bergmann	"Eating Light"
2009	Long	Geoffrey A. Landis	"Search"
	Short	Amal El-Mohtar	"Song for an Ancient City"
2010	Long	Kendall Evans and Samantha Henderson	"In the Astronaut Asylum"
	Short	Ann K. Schwader	"To Theia"
2011	Long	C. S. E. Cooney	"The Sea King's Second Bride"
	Short	Amal El-Mohtar	"Peach-Creamed Honey"
2012	Long	Megan Arkenberg	"The Curator Speaks in the Department of Dead Languages"
	Short	Shira Lipkin	"The Library, After"
2013	Long	Andrew Robbert Sutton	"Into Flight"
	Short	Terry Garey	"The Cat Star"
2014	Long	Mary Soon Lee	"Interregnum"
	Short	Amal El-Mohtar	"Turning the Leaves"

For a complete list of past Rhysling winners, runners-up, and nominees, see the Science Fiction Poetry Association archive at sfpoetry.com/ra/rhysarchive.html.

SFPA GRAND MASTER AWARD WINNERS

1999	Bruce Boston
2005	Robert Frazier
2008	Ray Bradbury
2010	Jane Yolen

HOW TO JOIN THE SFPA

Our members receive quarterly issues of *Star*Line*, the journal of the Science Fiction Poetry Association, filled with poetry, reviews, articles, and more. Members also receive a copy of the annual *Rhysling Anthology*, containing the best SF/F/H poetry of the previous year (selected by the membership), and *Dwarf Stars*, an edited anthology of the best short-short speculative poetry of the previous year.

Each member is allowed to nominate one short poem and one long poem to be printed in the *Rhysling Anthology* and then vote for the Rhysling Awards from the anthology. Members may nominate poems of ten lines or fewer to the *Dwarf Stars* editor and vote for that award as well. SFPA also sponsors the Elgin Awards for speculative poetry chapbooks and full-length books, and an annual poetry contest.

SFPA Membership – One Year
$15 • PDF only for Star*Line, Dwarf Stars, Rhysling Anthology
$30.00 • United States
$35.00 • Canada/Mexico
$40.00 • Overseas

Five Years
$60 • PDF only
$120 • United States
$140 • Canada/Mexico
$160 • Overseas

Lifetime
Payable in three payments over a period of three years.
$200 • PDF only
$450 • United States
$500 • Canada/Mexico
$550 • Overseas
(Failure to make all payments reverts membership to the number of years equivalent to the amount actually paid.)

All prices are in U.S. funds. Checks and money orders should be made out to the Science Fiction Poetry Association and sent to:

SFPA Treasurer
P.O. Box 907
Winchester, CA 92596

or pay online via PayPal to SFPATreasurer@gmail.com.

www.ingramcontent.com/pod-product-compliance
Lightning Source LLC
Chambersburg PA
CBHW070644050426
42451CB00008B/298